Collected Poems

Graham Rowlands

GRAHAM ROWLANDS

LYTHRUM PRESS
ADELAIDE

Published in 2009 by

Lythrum Press
PO Box 243 Rundle Mall
Adelaide SA 5000
Australia

www.lythrumpress.com.au

ISBN 978 1 921013 21 8

Cover design by Stacey Zass, Melbourne
Back cover portrait of Graham Rowlands by Jenni Mitchell
Designed and produced by Lythrum Press, Adelaide
Printed and bound by Hyde Park Press, Adelaide

National Library of Australia Cataloguing-in-Publication entry

Author:	Rowlands, Graham, 1947–
Title:	Collected poems / Graham Rowlands
ISBN:	978 1 921013 21 8 (pbk)
Dewey Number:	A821.3

Contents

1

2

3

Previous publications

Graham Rowlands has been publishing poems for over forty years. While his poetry has been published in several collections and widely anthologised, most of his poems first appeared in magazines, newspapers and journals. The following list is an indicative but not exhaustive list of previous publication.

Poems published in collections:

Stares and Statues, Makar Press, 1972

Replacing Mirrors, Saturday Centre, 1975

Poems Political, Makar Press, 1976

Adam Scolds, with Grahame Pitt and Lyndon Walker, Cochon International, 1976

Dial-A-Poem, Friendly Street Poets, 1982

On the Menu, Friendly Street Poets, 1988

Selected Poems, Wakefield Press, 1992

Poems first published in anthologies:

'The Museum of Atheism' in *Poems: Selected from The Australian's 20th Anniversary competition,* Judith Rodriguez and Andrew Taylor (eds), Angus and Robertson, 1985

'The Confidence Man' in *No. 13 Friendly Street Poetry Reader,* Constance Frazer and Barry Westburg (eds), Friendly Street Poets, 1989

'The Slang' in *Queensland: Words and all,* Manfred Jurgensen, Ed., Phoenix-Outrider, 1993

'The Laundries' in *No. 17 Friendly Street Poetry Reader,* Caroline Cleland and John Griffin (eds), Friendly Street Poets, Wakefield Press, 1993

'Osbert's Voyage' in *The Colonial Athens,* Martin R Johnson, Ed., Gawler Centenary of Federation Committee, 2001

'Don't Say' in *Vibrant: Poems and symposium papers presented at the Poetry and Poetics Symposium Adelaide 2007,* Guro Nygard and Nikki Carter (eds), Lythrum Press, 2007

Magazines, newspapers and journals in which poems have been published:

The Advertiser
The Age
Aspect
The Australian's Review of Books
Blast
Blue Dog
Broad Seat
The Bulletin
The Bunyip
The Canberra Times
Centoria
Compass
Coppertales
Cordite
The Courier-Mail
CRNLE Journal
Famous Reporter
Five Bells
Fling!
fourW
Going Down Swinging
Griffith REVIEW
Hobo
Image
Imago
Island
Larrikin
LiNQ
Mattoid
Meajin
The Mozzie
Muse
The Newcastle Herald
New England Review
Opinion
Overland
Page Seventeen
Patterns
Patterns/Broadsheet

Pendulum
The Phoenix Review
Poems Public
Poetry Australia
Poetry Monash
Prints
Quadrant
Redoubt
Salt-lick Quarterly
SideWaLK
The Small Times
Southerly
Southern Review
Spindrift
The Sydney Morning Herald
True North/Down Under
Ulitarra
Ultimate Ceasefire
Voices
The Weekend Australian
Westerly
Woorilla
Words
XTRA

Section 1

The Kite

My father bought me not
a diving & weaving kite but
a box kite that wasn't boxed but
wheeled, corrugated red plastic two-
wheeled on an axle of balsawood flaps.
Perhaps he didn't assemble it properly.
Perhaps the wind through the Norfolk pines
blew stronger through the headland pines
than he could have realised from the beach.
Probably he didn't say he'd hold the nylon
& I'd hold it after he'd held it or
then we'd hold it together for
as soon as the not-a-box kite spun
on its spindle in the blue salt air
it was airborne in a straight line of
whining whoosh up & out to sea-sky
in less than five seconds as we stared
colour into diminishing shape into nothing &
for twice as many seconds after nothing.

Sea Mullet

You kept your eyes open
for the fishermen's eyes open
for deep-sea mullet running
close to the sky, the coast.
You'd see the Jeeps tread sand
& the rowing boat unfold the net
& the professionals leaning
against the undertow, wet
in their cut-sleeve flannels.
Everyone helped. Everyone hindered.
Waves spawned patches of net
above the burying sand.
The pros didn't have to sell.
Still they sold for a song,
for silver – schooners.
Later, there seemed to be roe
fat as your thumb &
long as your longest finger
in every fish. You ate
the rich egg-grains of
millions of mullet.

Sunstroke

He would have taken out his inboard
without me, would have enjoyed himself
by himself. But I was the boss's son.
So we did the round of his crabpots.

There were a few mud crabs. Probably.
I don't remember. After half an hour
in the boat in the sun in January
I didn't 'feel well' & so I had to put
my wrists in the water to cool my blood
& then I had to lie under the canvas.
There were whiting & flathead to catch.

I lay on the bed in the spare room
wanting to vomit but not vomiting
wanting to sleep but not sleeping
not wanting to live but living.

Not dams, not lakes, not fjords but
all flat water is my first flat water –
all flat water wide open to the sea.

The Neighbours

Jack was the son of John and Mrs G
who renamed him John II, although John
still called him Jack until his dotage.
Mrs G told one almost blind grandmother
her roses were cyclamen. Not red. See?
Mr G was called an old Chink by a fruit-seller.
Mrs G laughed. Others also laughed because,
being bald, he looked like an old Chinaman.
John-Jack was thought to be odd, most odd
because he didn't swear or play football.
G's gate read: NO HAWKERS, PLEASE.
And John-Jack never married.

Adolph and Mrs P were Jehovah's Witnesses who
Jehovahed two of their three daughters
into tramping all over the city –
Witnessing. They must have seen a few things.
Aged twenty, the other rolled in drunk one night
& Mr P apologised next day to the neighbours
for belting his Hell-bound daughter who still
qualified as medico & married an alcoholic patient
who died not long after of medicinal purposes.

For good reasons Mr & Mrs K almost changed
their K to C during World War II. After,
they had their big son James, their Jimmy
who converted piping into a bike &
half a rubbish dump into his deadly
hotrod pranging manglebar. After
Mr K became Commissioner of Transport
he laid his own concrete driveway. Jimmy
was last seen pinning his father's shoulders
to their back lawn after wrestling lessons.
He ended up in life insurance.

When Mrs B had a daughter Mr B stopped talking
to her, moved sofa & bedding downstairs, ate
every evening meal without looking at her
while continuing to provide housekeeping fives.
No matter how accidentally, he fathered
a shy, slow-learning, late-developing child
whose long silences were not totally
unconnected with his own stoic solitude.
He died walking up a neighbour's front steps,
out of breath, apparently about to speak.

George Helverson

George Helverson
pursed his lips
as he spoke
on
bowling
batting
fielding
umpiring
on scoring
with the scheme he'd devised –
Helverson's Simplified Scoring Scheme
& since we were all men
at his lecture
a word
about –
protectors.
Out to his car he'd go
every once in a while
during lessons
to hear
someone or
someone else's
long runup from the Northern end
& over & oh a good deal of
movement through the air
on that ball &
in his class loud
as late Saturday afternoon
in the outer
near the bar &
a stonewalling batsman.
Hell-of-a-son
George Hell-of-a-son
said someone eleven years old
but George went on umpiring &
scoring away

on his Scheme of things
placid, imperturbable
until one boy said
Jeez
look at the bum on that dame.
George raised his arm
& stopped the bowler
on his way in
from the lavatory end &
deliberately turning around
he slowly pursed his lips & said:
Please, not bum – buttocks.

The Swimming Lesson

We dipped through the disinfectant
out of the swimming pool's changerooms.
Halt. One of us hadn't been to the loo,
under the sprinkler or through the feet dip.
The instructor wanted to know how the boy
coped with his daily ablutions – which
he didn't understand, of course, never
being meant to be more than a dunce
by courtesy of public interrogation
beside a green pool under a blue sky,
school and church on the hill.

Now put your fingers between your toes
instructed the instructor of sport and drama.
Now, rub. Rub harder. Harder. Urgently. Go on.
The grubbings rubbed into long black tobacco.
Twenty years ago. The Good Old Days.

You Don't Fit into Metric

A long day's looking over my shoulder into
last night's dream of – of all people, you.
Eighteen years since I last saw you.
A decade since *anyone* last saw you.
Piss off, you old bastard. Piss off.
All six feet six of you. You don't
fit into metric any easier than you
fitted into a standard bed or coffin.
Yours was on special order, I suppose –
although, if the lid wouldn't go down,
it was no doubt some like-minded Old Boy
who bribed the Funeral Director's apprentice
to stick your last test tube up your arse.

The honours I honoured you with (you & the school;
I couldn't dishonour father & mother without you)
weren't the mile, the butterfly, the First Eleven –
were words, words you couldn't get your tongue around.
You hated to, but you had to announce them.
I always won. If only I'd been someone else.

When you expelled me in my own dream
(That was your dream too, of course)
I could only race away in slow motion
through your rows of eyes right, eyes right,
your jungle training nets, your 303s –
your troops lined up for World War III.

Still, perhaps you *were* a harmless old coot
blithering, blathering, blimping away
way beyond your rows of chemicals.
Everyone said so, of course – later.

I could out-quote you. Out-argue you.
Even at sixteen, I'd out-read you. So why
don't you piss off, you old bastard.

You still scare me shitless.

One Teacher

Don't be Yes-men. Have principles. Make some enemies,
he advised, urging us on to be nothing but ourselves –

to be miserable young Hamlets and Lord Jims, if necessary,
two hopeless cases who had to die for our matriculation.

Even so, he stirred all quite demented Hamlets To be
not not to be – only not to be too willing Lord Jims

apologising to the powers-that-used-to-be for boys set
to act in, act out, to be both Hamlet and Lord Jim.

Call it hero-worship. I didn't then. I do now call it
something more or less than Hamlet and Lord Jim.

This one teacher understood how fathers shouldn't
couldn't claim to be or be Lords or Princes –

one teacher himself neither Hamlet nor Lord Jim.
Because he was not my father, I loved him.

Marking Secondary School Papers

Surfies paddle out their boards,
furrow down a breaker
waving their last good-bye to rules, to me,
thumbing a nose or two.
They're off to groove their way, their waves.
They're different but they're through.
How just I am.

Forty, fifty, sixty papers mirror me
as I pass a former self a hundred times,
precocious, pithy, full of spite.
Good on them, good marks.

What can I do, though, with one word-hater
unable to hate in words?
Down back streets with hard knuckles,
broken bottles, drunken breath,
he'd teach teacher more than school.
Rape for women, scars for men, for me,
I imagine the perfection of his muscles' style.

I fail him as he stutters out
his impotence and rage.

Fred Hoyle's Bjelke

Influenza is caused by comets seeding the earth with viruses.
– Fred Hoyle

Out among your rows of peanuts, Joh,
you're praying for rain again
to a sky's dry blue.

Comets you can't see, Joh, seed, Joh, seed
the upper reaches of atmosphere full of
disease tumbling down turbulence

& into raindrops often raining smaller
droplets of life wriggling
out of a comet.

In dry times they're dropped by evaporating
raindrops & sprinkled through the air
like weevils out of flour.

We're counting on Fred Hoyle's comets, Joh,
to bring you down, Joh,
with influenza.

The Ex-Queenslanders

There's only one thing worse than a Queenslander.
An ex. There are *n* number of exs carrying their
little icons of nostalgia south south south
south-west, even popping up in other hemispheres –
those with photographs sealing them in albums,
those without, miraging their memories with high
mirrorball-less ballrooms ballroom-less ballrooms;
lovely old verandahs they've only seen on television;
trade union bunkers where trade union heavies
fought off revolution for a knight, a knighthood;
the Away, away, with rum, by gum People's Palace
entered at your own risk of Bible-reading, praying,
crying, crying *War Cry* & playing the trombone forever –
unable to handle either the alcohol *or* the air
at well over .08 insecticide .08 disinfectant.
It doesn't matter whether you walked a long slow last
walk across the walkway of the high grey bridge &
decided Queensland wasn't worth it (dying, not living)
or whether you put everything you ever owned to the
torch of a bonfire on your very last night here,
inviting a cast of, well, one or two, a handful
or whether you slipped out, shot through, pissed off
thinking, who cares, she's only a Queenslander.
Later, when *you're* only a Queenslander again (briefly)
you blossom into frangipanni, poinciana, poinsettia
& the aesthetics of fruit & vegies at the (Joh yes!)
District Exhibits, The Exhibition, Brisbane. August.

Me? I'm a bloody Queenslander & I'm bloody proud
I loathe Queensland. Loathe. Why shouldn't I?
I've *felt* the thin blue line's stiff arm.
I've *seen* the expressways through & over & out.
The bulldozers scrape. The wreckers' balls, ball.
(Or at least I've seen Progress – in the morning.)
I've voted. I've argued. I've shouted. I've marched.
Joh yes! Joh *no!* I've chanted. I've yelled. I've failed.

The Sirs

The Sirs are going. Yes Sir
the Sirs following in their Sirs' footsteps;
the Sirs recommended by Sirs to Sir & Sirred by Sir &
the Sirs recommending themselves to Sir & Sirred by Sir
Sir having been Sirred by a Sir (if not sired
by a Sir) on the recommendation of Sirs;
allowing for one-off Sirs (Sir Galahads)
the Sirs of Honour among Sirs, yes Sir, those Sirs
the shady, the shifty, the dodgy, the dicey
including the Sirs no longer Sirs
(neither all the dead Sirs nor
the Sirs just managing to be dead
Sirs while still Sirs). Yes Sir
the Sirs are going.

Section 2

Zarathustra in a Jet

A paranoid pilot at the controls.
'God is Dead.' flaunted in sky-writing
over the cemetery of a bombed-out city.
Somewhere, either on the recruiting poster,
during the medical check or at the briefing,
something went wrong … click
in the mind or on the instrument panel,

something snapped.
After the final word, the D, the dot
came the second coming, Zarathustra in a jet.
With face and controls set,
he sighted the automatic pilot to the target
nose down, flaps left as they were.
Then he dived for the cathedral.

Void

All things turn on a hollow centre:
bud folds on itself, opening red
in a burning point of fire, beginning
going back to the vacuum of beginning –
petals diminished within themselves, flames
alight around a bud-centre of air.

Cyclone turns on a still cone;
planets unwind in spirals
out of the catherine wheel of a nebula
as it frays in trailing sparks
from a centre of nothing.

All human consolation:
organ pipes blowing bubbles of sound
from long silver columns;
and man, with the artistry of a glass blower
working his tube between the grip of life,
the taut opening of a woman,
as fluid moves, fountaining hot, hollow
through him, into the final void.

Roles

Authorities organise, order the world.
Animals enter the Ark as a comic strip
of breeding monkeys breathing life into men.
Although a mutant thumb is pure chance
they know the brain forms to know itself.

Stars swarm like plankton for them
enfolded petals of anemone open
as animals feed on one another,
breathing as one organism.
At the centre of circling rings of matter, omega point.

Whether I am free to choose or not,
I play the role of hero.
I will not submit.
I mourn the passing of lumbering brontosaurus
wrestling with, sinking in mud,
long columns of bone
building a first temple of the swamps.
I mourn life starved from amoeba,
spawn of jelly too small to see.

I mourn a ghetto collapsed to saltpan of bricks
while only a border, a religion or a race apart,
echoes, hollow, the silence of the Domes.

The Christs

Christ knows! There are too many Christs
for Christ's sake should be singular
Christ unique Christ numero uno Christ.

There are Christ knows how many Christs crucified
& crucifixed in plaster casts by the tonne
rattling along on trolleys at the Vatican.

You don't have to unroll the Dead Sea Scrolls
to find the first Coming of Christ – Australian
novelists are always crucifying some poor Christ.

Every generation re-Christens its own Christs:
Jeez! Christ Almighty! Jesus F. Christ! (He's American.)
You can no longer blaspheme so many blasphemies.

There are God Squad Christs riding Shinto Yamahas
on crusades against the Skull & Crossbones on Kawasakis.
The God Squad carry only their Cross, paint & stencil.

There are lime green flying Christs like neon signs
who can dive through walls & tombstone doors – immune
to death & kryptonite & believing in Everlasting Art:

these luminous kites hanging around in orange skies.
The Vatican will sell brass to hang them in the Sistine
one thousand millennia after the last Easter joke.

Suffering Christ & behold! Only the Anti-Christ.
Suffering Christs & behold! You have Christ knows
Christs know how many insufferable Anti-Christs.

First Communion

The body of Christ doled out disembodied

always white confetti, white tiddlywinks,
white half-pennies pressed out of wallpaper

tasting of Absolutely nothing dissolving
in the leanest pickings on earth.

I think I tasted my first alcohol
there, watered down, in my first wine.

If the wafer had been a juicy rump steak
done medium to rare in the sun's blood

or T-bone passed from teeth to teeth
blowing away green crystals of flies –

the stain of black into purple mulberries
from the tree next to the church

wouldn't have been the only stigmata on my hands.

Getting Religion

I believe in the miracle of garbage collection every Wednesday,
in the separation of bottles from wrapped-up food scraps
in many thicknesses of thick paper around jagged glass
in seafood waste in the freezer until Tuesday night. Amen.
My faith didn't disappear with the disappearing white truck
in the sacrilege of that night I forgot the garbage &
faith or duty or common sense set me running after the garbos,
brown plastic bin in one hand, orange plastic bin in the other
following magic or mystery or the carnivorous white truck.
When I caught up & tipped in the bins I saw or thought I saw
the light of a star-shaped *blancmange* eaten by a black hole.

I believe in gas & water & electricity & the organs of my body
with the same devotion to ritual & regularity (& ignorance)
that I devote to the collection of garbage every Wednesday.
From the very moment the wave of some laser wand turned
that *blancmange* into a vanishing star I knew there'd be
no need for miracles. Ripeness would be all. All, miraculous.
All would be eternally beyond understanding & understood.
If I crash in the Andes or just in the northern Flinders
I know without any scruple, any churning of the stomach
I'll eat the just dead passengers one by just dying one
in a worship that eats their body & blood like gods.
Then I'll wait for my own disciples. Let us pray:
Blancmange, my lambs.

Magician and Philosopher

Love life more than the meaning of it? – Ivan Karamazov

I wave a pen, dip my wand in stardust
over my hat, a red-lined bowler of a lucky dip.
With a turn of the hand on a spotted scarf
I show the audience opals and crystals
I show them sun flecks
on the long hair of the woman I loved,
and I show them shadows.

I see words more than people
and people only through the words, their meaning:
I take the letters of some type-setter,
see pattern in a crossword of alphabet
and turn them into neon signs
looped high above the cities.

I know that the sequin inlays
on a peacock's tail
are devoid of meaning
and that nothing is less real,
more real, than words.

Just Scared?

To live, he thinks to himself
even if every sphere of philosophy turns to ellipse
and the bones of an argument
won't take the sway of a young back
or curve back the other way of an old spine;

living, even if X-ray of his eyes
turns footballers to gladiators
and a stadium to a colosseum,
or only to see a stone fist of defiance
exhumed from the burial of its own prediction;

living and outliving
the philosophy of pride in looking in a mirror
at himself, at nothing
but the pride of facing nothing
as the meaning of the lightning streak and of the snail.

Or does he know, even as he doesn't do it,
that he's been scared of going over the cliff?

The Not Nothing Poem

Think of the three minute universe
without the four minute mile or
the nine second apology

& you're on your way to the
anti-similes anti-metaphors of the anti-poem –
the emu that can be or be like
a gorilla a balloon a tricycle
but not an ostrich.

The anti-poem is still the poem.

Neither the pitiless nor the penniless –
only you poemless
blissfully
don't discover the knowhow & why of
the beginning of
everything

don't find anything out there
to be or be like
anything here.

You who've never rhymed a rhyme
a slang or a nursery rhyme
sprung a rhythm
freed a verse
porned a wall –

only you blissfully know nothing

about the beginning of everything
in the time capsule you'll
never unearth:

between sometime & somewhere
in timelessness & spacelessness
somehow time knitted with space
a pinprick a bubble a tennis ball
a hole full of whole families of
nimble electrons & their relatives
living together with quarks
shy now in the nuclei of atoms
but in the public cyclone Cyclops eye
(I think, therefore we were)
in the quark era (I think we were)
followed by the taming of the wild quarks
owing nothing to Ibsen or Shakespeare
cooling cooling yea cooling until
setting themselves up
in irresistible threesomes &
woe betide one who tries to leave.

The Neighbour's Angel

From his cherry picker, the tree removalist
zipped all the branches off the silver birch &
then his off-sider zapped the silver-white trunk.
Vines, shrubs & bushes came down & out by hand
just before they could turn their last autumn.
A picket fence unfolded like a paper cut-out.

Then something landed. Lo. Was it an angel?
Surely not in a birdbath. It couldn't be.
It was. I hate, I have always hated angels.
Perhaps an angel swooped up towards me out of
Sunday School's crypt, a pedophile with wings.
No evidence at all, of course, would prove it.
Later, I shot the angels out of *Paradise Lost.*
A pity I hadn't opened a page of John Milton.
So, in Europe, I was on my best behaviour. I
let angels wing their way out of the centuries
to be stilled in mosaic, fresco, stained glass
& wasn't I surprised to find sly & bi faces.

Why on earth, then, am I up here on the roof?
No, not bird-watching – despite my binoculars.
Oh no, no, not that. What do you take me for?
True, I'm no angel. I dent the corrugated iron.
But neither is the angel an angel. It's a cherub.

The Original

There, sometimes, in the mirror
you find your opposite – everything
you don't believe in &
still you

those firsts
the ballbearing
the golfball in the typewriter

imperfect only by imitation & patent

& so, somewhere,
in ice or under sand, you'll
bury a ballbearing
studded with a
new alphabet of
a poem

the original of
no others

anonymous & anonymously

for no-one to find

as if, somehow, you're not god.

Section 3

From Either Side

Two bodies lay sculpted flat between pages,
grained by a photograph in miniature.
Through the months of love with a woman
I saw their lips grow close together,
large bodies strain, curling
curving one into the other,
how the soft furrow of her back arched to meet love
while his neck strained
from a shoulder-blade knotting his skin.

For old time's sake, we went
to the gallery, to the figures
that had lived large for me in dream.
How they were reduced to the measure of bronze
that rippled before us, sinewing smoother than flesh
as the hand cupped on her slender thigh.

Mincing around tiny forms on the stand
we, connoisseurs of the cold flesh holding,
body folding into body.
We, peeping under arms, over shoulders,
looking from either side to each other,
separated by naked limbs
that mocked us –
two lovers, two statues cast from different moulds.

Infidelity

What is your memory of a woman?
A composite of times, a dozen slides of women
beamed together onto a screen, all blurred?

Is it the act of devotion to one?
What an odd spool unwinds through your mind:
the day the red strap on her swimsuit broke
and a hair whiskered out from nylon – where?

Why won't Mount of Venus on the pillow stay in shape,
the satin bedspread resist your hand?
Fickle mistress!

When images sprocket past your eye faster
can't you hold, can't you keep some moment of her
in the white evening gown,
tight necklace round her throat?

No – taut string breaks,
beads spill across the floor.
This, your first infidelity.

Doughnuts

Squeezed and puffed and paddled around in oil –
doughnuts
slipped down the dip
onto flat metal trays shuttled along rails –
doughnuts done to a turn.

Your life, the women tell you in a clipped word
circles on the same wheels every time.
Your freedom is the freedom of the slide.
Even that's planned.

So, just to spite them
you stop at a roadside stall somewhere with
A dozen please.
But are they doughnuts
those flat oozing flaps of batter?

You must be different from the rest.
Still, you have to pay and coins
flip in the same circles every time.

So they roll you in sugar,
twirl you around a few times, slide you
into the open bag, twisting the paper ears,
as they hand you over
to the first customer coming by.

Elusive

You are too elusive for them, snake
slithering out of last year's fashions,
your cellophane self crinkled on the ground.

You slide so easily out of clothes for them.
Is it a rite, a ritual
this search for yourself
curving under them, coiling round, corded
together in strands of a rope?

Is your nerve of being sinewed in your flesh,
fibred too deep for men to unravel?
All you can do is ease sinuously
through yourself
and slough them off.

Moment of Loss

Even when you care about the woman
there is a moment
when necks cease to chafe,
teeth ungritting on quick gulps of air.

That is the sprawl across her body,
slippery on damp breasts,
when your tongue through her lips
feels its own taste

when, even for the woman,
the serpent of Eden will be
papier-mâché
elongated with empty air,
now that pressure is within.

Yet, if it is not both of you
is it all your own?
Or is there the force-funnelled moment of loss
when final selfishness,
when the egoism of the designer
draws him into a wind tunnel?

Days

Small crabs scuttle on the beach, scatter
like marbles spilled from a bag
as we slip down sand hills.
They always run away.

Sometimes, we, the two of us,
chafe against each other, hand in hand,
as we slide down a damp crease
in the wind-folded dunes.

I feel I cannot resist,
I resent this sand.

Prince Charming

I have problems with Prince Charming.
I haven't seen him yet but
know he's in bed with us
because his white doublet hangs
like a ghost from my coat-hanger.
His stockings drape the chair,
cross-garters on the floor
next to my jeans and black belt.

The zip is to blame,
I'm too fast for her
while his dozens of buttons
allow them to move easily, both at once.
I have to resist an urge to be slow,
to be him, Prince Charming, the fop.

I suppose I should be grateful
she needs me to reach him
among the moonlight and roses.

Mirrors

He thinks she won't like them
but she does, the bare-breasted women
who must have posed a hundred times
to reach the certain glare and pout
that would sell the magazine.
She imagines herself as them.

Later, they both pose before the mirror
each watching, wanting
the other stranger in the glass
as men and women on a screen.

She, by herself, is not enough.
She wants to feel herself and him at once
wanting, finally, her girlhood self again
sheathed in net and tourniqueted in scarves
wearing bracelet, ring and bands
as her body moves against her body
until she and the act are one.

The Need

She would come to him a dozen times a day,
cry sometimes, berate herself as worthless
or pout his lack of concern until she had her way.
She would come to him in anger,
unfold his rug across the floor and wait, spreadeagled,
to slash his back with nails.
She would run away from him at parties
because of lack or praise, and,
because she couldn't mould him to her moods,
she left him, saying
that he humbled, controlled, he owned her.
The need was simpler: other men.

Yet, either she tired or they
as she lay smouldering, sullen, unfulfilled,
until, in dream or nightmare,
under force of hurricane or earthquake,
she met her childhood self returning
and her burning thirst was slaked only when she rose,
arching her back, roused on pillows of fire
to take the weight of Satan.

Jazz Ballet

Sixteen & jazz ballet
in black dancing tights
bronze miniskirt &
twenty-three, myself.

Jazz ballet & all the arts. Well then
would she like to see my *sculptural* painting?
(Didn't own an etching.)
Yes, she'd love to.
What did it mean? Ummmmmm … well … maybe.
Anyway, there's this exhibition at Square O.
Oh! She was sorry. Jazz ballet.
Oh well.

Saturday night. 11pm.
This knock & vodka & vermouth & potato wafers
& stuffed olives & cheese & biscuits – all stolen
from some party & jazz ballet
in a long green dress she'd designed
herself. Oh! She didn't
want to disturb me
in her slightly French accent
that didn't last long.

Jazz ballet is trapeze in bed.

For what was left of Sunday
I shot the broken centreline through us
like bullets off bitumen & on
towards ocean combers too cold
for surfing & back to her sister's
for new clothes (I don't know what for)
& back to me & back to her sister's
after more jazz ballet &
Toodle-oo!

& should have left it at that.

That's All

Now you're alone in bed
twisting between rumpled sheets.

Fool, you still want her
although she was a chance meeting
by a rockpool in the river.
She ran off, you followed
(men always have to try)
until you saw her move
between dark boles and boulders near water.

Even at a short distance from you
she seemed no more than shadow;
and you, a peeping tom through the ferns.

When she ran out of the pool
you knew she must be naked
before you felt her wet skin
slippery against your own,
her hair clinging to her sway back,
nipples like sultanas in your hands.

That's all. She'll phone in the morning,
breaking her promise with a headache or a cold.

Climax

As if opposition to the very act
allowed the way to action,
their own parodies
they lay in bouncing bed
toe to toe, poet to poet,
not for art's sake
or to release strain
too strenuously imposed
by censorship or contraception,
until the Moving Finger,
the Muse, the White Goddess
the What-You-Will
in which neither believes,
until climax rocked the book-ended bed
knocked them unconscious
locked them spine with spine,
immortals, though dead.

Magic

She, who ate men, raw, ate him
didn't eat him
ate him. He remained.
Mars was plasma. Membrane nebulae.
Cold ball-bearings grew red fire
as she took his world
into her, transfused
shake and stutter
with her raw nerve
and vitamins.

The latter, her tough self. Informed. Intelligent.
Brutal critic, barbarous backtalk
her fencing poise, pose,
while on her feet.

For the rest, witch, gipsy, sorceress,
fortuneteller, conjurer with words
she links thing with thing.
They merge. She works through blood.
Not quite black, the magic
neither is budded staff.
She contracts, he grows
larger and larger
until he thinks, he feels
if now
then half of him goes. Blows.

Entrances

He knew he wouldn't be alone
when he entered, they walked
arm in arm inside, she'd
never leave him be

once they canoed by slipstream's water
updown through cave's mouth
into her dreamscape words
where she fed the animals

he shared her with bat, bird, flyingfox,
another one of her animals
unable to fly or fear
lion's pride, tiger's stripe.

Buffaloes stamped hooves at her
before she excised tongues lovingly
with stoneknife pared by stone. Blood dripping
she stripped, salted meat to dry.

When grapes ripened purple for winepress red
she severed every animal throat;
with bear, ermine, mink skins
closed off cavemouth's glare.

Meteors flared down javelin paths
shrieked redwhite tracery arcs
at eggs and moons laid
in woven nest of witch's hair.

Bees hived honey in her ears, swarmed
trails out of hearing, left her
to hibernate and suckle pup, calf, eggs,
where she was winter spring and the world.

Hail melted on her forehead as dew
birthsweat mothered whales in ovaries
wild comets veered from her eyes, their tails
turned silkthread gestating genes and species.

Feared shapes he could father
shuddered through him, he she
aborted in movement of earth's crust.
She cast no spell, released him.

If she squeezed him easy from her thighs
and he risked no rips to vanity, he
must have woken a world away from dream
forgotten everything but unexplained loss
at entrances once entered never again.

Karma

First I could because I didn't
love her & was pleased
despite & because of

that being the reverse of
only supposed to
if I did
love &

even that supposed to be hallowed
sealed & delivered
before delivery.

Then I thought I couldn't because
of this other woman
but sure I didn't
love I was
okay

although on a couple of occasions
I'd have to admit it was
a bit awkward.

Then the most extraordinary happened
the ordinary that keeps on
happening to everyone

although it was resisted &
new to me &
scary &

I was forced to admit it
was love & I didn't
like love at
all but

it was love & I guess
it wasn't entirely
unlinked with

the fact that on a particular day
at a particular moment at an
unexpected meeting with
this other woman

she'd (I mean this other woman)
she'd (I hated to say it
to myself let alone
to her) vanished.

It was not a third person we'd invented
& I don't think it was
a third person I'd
invented but
if it was

then it was she & she could only
be this other woman's woman
out of this other woman
made by & for me
& anyway

we were both alone together in a crowd
(we being this other woman & I)
trying to talk to each other
because she knew I
had this thing
about her &

although she no longer had a thing
about me she was trying to
be nice to me & I
to her I think
or hope
I was

but we were finding the going &
staying pretty difficult.

So I guess that the absence of
this thing I once called
love only once

meant if not some reincarnation
on the old karma then
the equivalent:

because I was once again in love
(tra la la & dumpty dee &
it looks as if it's
for good)

I knew I'd find & did
find for a while I
couldn't with
her

(not this other woman).

Openspace

Without a room of my own
I hunch down over my desk
as I take another phone call.
I pronounce my name & section.
She pronounces her name & subject
& already they're more than enough to
lengthen my on-the-job 10 am into a
long autumn afternoon filled with
the pale yellow of her ever so
slow singsong singsonging up &
down the line to me & down & up
into pins & needles in my head.
It wouldn't take me long to flip
to her capital letter & surname but
only her exact age would be of interest
because I know there's nothing young
in the voice. I don't want to know.
When I would offer my lady anything
at all, I can offer only my soft oohs
ahs, oh nos & you-don't-says
to slow & lengthen the flow of
honey pale as near-winter sun
down the full length of
my spine.

Section 4

The Early 1950s

When my father arrived home from work
he used to upend his grey trousers &
coins flipped & rolled everywhere
copper & silver out of
his fob pocket
for me to pick up & keep.

I watched where he kept his wallet &
once I stole a ten shilling note &
took it to school in a matchbox
I papered with wallpaper for
my seven year old flame
who turned me on &
turned me in.

On the same day a pound note disappeared &
I was asked question after question
that was always the same question
about the ten shilling note –
was it one of two?

The Acting Head got the Headmaster's cane &
caned himself five times on the hand
before flicking it at me &
phoning my mother to ask
whether or not
she was going to have
more children

which she found impertinent.

Shadows

I grew in my mother's shadow
very small at first, then taller
as if she walked at night
under lights spaced evenly apart.

Later, when she read me a story
about wicked pixie's sharpened ears
I did not, could not see cruel points of satire
when elf snipped off people from their shadows.

It was years before I gripped scissors
and then, I could not cut
I had to tear.

Lives

As the elegant table-leg of the eagle
holds a ball in its talons
so my parents are mirrored there,
held in a fine polish of furniture.

I must mince over the carpet, not walk,
only to be received by disdaining arms of a chair.
Though light is dimmed in cones nearby
I will not reach their quality, cannot
live up to the measure of their room.

I wish them well but far away.
I, with a mania for volcanoes,
for the principle of life and death they hold;
I, who see in orange lava below the crust
my hot fluid self burning,
moving and burning alive in my skin.

Twenty-one Years

Twenty-one singles fold in my hand,
one for each year.
Filing a thumb nail down crisp edges
I feel what this means to them:
neat icing on cake, a large silver key,
my name tastefully scrolled.

Why do those few minutes late
burn down my throat when I swallow?
Is it how little I cared for the party, saying,
it was theirs, not mine,
cinnamon sprinkled, hazel-nuts cracked
to some ideal of their own, saying,
any number of years is an arbitrary date?

For me, a duty to be done –
polish on my black shoes, not a brush to my suede;
polite replies to a hundred banalities
mouthed by relatives among memories of their own
lived years before I was born.

A long glass stems between fingers, opening
to rim circled pink with sugar:
a brandy crusta cooling my hand
that chafed raw between the grip of parents
when I lived at home with them, alone.

Twenty-one years lie in those pounds of raisins,
in the cake standing on lace cloth.
Icing smooths over bumps.
Knife slips through layers
to chorus of wrinkled throats, raucous;
no speech from me, not even a request.
So little could be said; so much omitted.

With relations gone,
crumbs brushed from the table,
I drink the last flat champagne,
saying my thanks with a sincerity
that could never be acted.
My mother, eyes moist, says
in the elegance of their dining room,
she hopes I wasn't bored.

Magic Carpet to Europe

I take the armchair ride around Europe
in my parents' living room as
liner, plane, train, hovercraft
spirit me through three hours' slides
on family reunion's magic carpet.

What guides think in native tongues
about people always finding like-minded people nice,
dollars flourished and the English language
easiest to follow when drawled,
guides tell only to wives in bed.

My parents review views re-ride skyway rides
repeat after each other (as if say after me)
places, towns, villages, nations that aren't enough.
I must find words, ahs, gasps beyond words
for each new vista's Isn't it beautiful.

Alpine goatherds are long since postcard
although I value their not being
towers, steps, manicured hedgerows
too beautiful roses' geometry
set in patterned beds like magic,
the whim of some royal tyrant.
Europe's history. No thread or petal out of place.

And back to 11 pm coffee, datepies,
via Singapore's steamed white buildings
impeccably clean streets, progress, future.
I'm made to feel my hair's too long and Mussolini
worked hard to set the trains on time.

Home to Mother

Wrong again.
Because he'd gone for natural foods,
the Christmas cake would sweat into mould
after a few weeks of humid heat,
homemade biscuits the same way.
Wrong again,
not enough beer for his friends
because all hers drank shandies
and after two, no more
for a lifetime.
Like beer, like the uprooted garden
from a half-lost afternoon
when he brought home a schoolfriend
whose dog took to the neatly seeded annuals.

Wrong again, he wouldn't fight
because he'd fly off in eleven days,
exhilarate, jet-lift over the cool apartment
fringed with frangipani.
Lazy and rebellious (both, Mother dear?)
he'd done it this time,
brought them home in long hair
after a lapse of years
for tellers and salesmen to catch up.
After insult and nag
after doing things not needing done
blackmail
should have
wrenched a guilty kiss from ingratitude.
But she was wrong again.

Fashions

Pupils will dilate in old age
when everything else's done for
only remaining adolescent urge
all your life looking for
whatever they're called by then
larger than life that's
sometimes no exaggeration
you've been through titties
tits breasts norks boobs and knockers
you've seen the upswung 1950s
downturn to sizes fitting everyone
but outmoded colossi always
in vogue for someone.

You saw them swing back to anything
goes braless in nipple winter.
Years folded unfolded them
down the cleavage of
round the flattened knolls of
history that's also your mother
in bed eating biscuit
sodden with milky tea
your father brought, the most
he was allowed to do and you
just challenging his authority
nothing oedipal in bosoms
you home in for at eighty.
Two breasts make one bosom.
Remember that from your mother.

The Geode

Found,
whole, uncut –
only a rough ball of rock
tracing red oxide through pitted grey-white.

Found,
cut open, open-cut –
only one twin half a geode – although
inside grey-white finding
a jagged band of
olive & sepia agate running black
around the outer edge & brown around the inner
set against grey-blue outlining of
the empty centre lined
with quartz crystals
too old to be
amethyst
& only once on the boil
swelling inside lava, swelling lava.

To split
to split out of
this geode – to be, to be born
an immaculate conception
without a mother.

Fathers

Santa Claus, my father, arrived with toys
on Christmas Eves, stayed for days of hours
spent coaching me cricket,
teaching me to kick the same football he kicked.

Both father and son moved on springs.
First he'd give coins for the slot;
I'd press knobs for silver balls to rise.
We lined our teams up straight,
faced each other, both said Go.

In my study, though,
I built another father out of books:
a dozen characters from novels
I poured into my mould,
junk sculpture, a gallery of painted faces,
until my father met my father in my room.

They wrestle, two rivals in my mind;
both fathers and sons create their Frankensteins.

Willpower

For both explanation and excuse
my father never forgot the chaff bags.
In his parents' house they served as towels.
Youngest, privileged son of a large, poor family,
even when he made the grade in real estate and law
he couldn't stop. He remodelled blocks of flats.
He planted pineapples for canneries and tax deductions.

Some similar energy turns the pages
of my thousand books: unable to do, I teach
that words and thoughts are action too. Prissy. Precise.
Though my father now regrets his denigration
he would be surprised to learn
I am still my father's son.

I enter a gabled hotel.
Below the broken coat of arms
a fire blazes in the marble fireplace.
The high ceiling arches, aristocratic.
I sip my drink, tempted;
resolve not to buy the place.
I am determined not to make a million.

Investiture

The king who was not born to royalty
who never had kingship thrust upon him,
achieved distinction of his own defining.

Despising crown and emblem and garter
he wore no deep robes of ritual,
looked to lineage not of his own line.

His sword was sheathed from sun and jewel
in the presence of flattery's courting
as he engaged the enemy and the jester.

The former was a trial of royalty's strength
and, looking down on sycophancy as if king,
the enemy drew king's blood in duelling.

Swordplay did not threaten the throne
but even outrageous courage could dare
beyond the gamble and test of indulgence.

The king ordered banishment of his enemy,
dismissed all his silk and velvet flatterers
but the motley of his patient jester

who would never say treason to the crown
but play subtle games endangering favour
with their humour far too funny

who would not hint at the king's neglect
but encircle the throne with complaints,
never sparing the enemy verbal daggers.

He never mentioned the rivalry of siblings
on horseback in the lists or over goblets
clinked golden to the plunder of victory

and with no thought of capital crimes
from blasphemy against realms of ancient sky,
the jester rejected Lord and Father

and knelt even as he would not kneel
for the sword on both his shoulders
and rose knight although still jester

and said without a word: my father.

One of My Last Letters to My Father

It might not be.
There could be many more
imitations of imitations of imitations
required of me by
him & me.

By now
he would be
surprised if I gave up & gave in &
not so sure I wasn't
lying.

So I sign-off
as I've signed-off all the others
with the most common of
four-letter words

the one I don't believe
a letter of.

The Pies

Augie Sauer's pies. They don't
make pies like that any more.
By Jove he could make pies.

They were 'twenty years ago'
then, but only 300 miles away
& a walk down the street.

My word he could make pies.
They *tasted* better. They had to.
I'd heard so much about them.

So I bought I don't know
how many – with 'their' money &
packed them as if I'd made them

layer on cardboard layer
in the small oven of a
shoebox tied with string

& flew them 300 miles home
as hand luggage in a DC3 &
'they' were pleased, I thought.

It was only later, much later
that they'd always found it funny
& hey! wasn't it (nudge nudge) funny?

Even now they wonder why I
think I'm too grown up
to be bothered with Christmas.

They're Proud

Ah! They're proud of me.
Every five years or so, a friend
of a friend's friend tells me so.

I've never forgotten the scowl
she gave me when I cracked only
73% in my first public exam
abolished a few years after.
She was a failure, I was
a failure because I
failed to make 90%.
But they were still
proud I'd done my best.
Someone told me so
at least twenty years after.

I heard I was bignoted
once at the school's
fund-raising-in-a-big-tent-appeal
for Old Boys to pass on
their privilege to
privilege. *They*
never told me. Although
they hated what I was doing
they must have been proud
I was doing it well.

It's quite possible
they're still proud of me:
I don't know, I no longer
read their letters & I'm
not going to their funerals.

The Parting

Her room wasn't quite a hospital's.
Sheets sewn with the nursing home's brand
weren't terminal. No sign spelt Infirmary.

Maid, maiden, old maid, she encouraged
others to the patter of little feet.
Perhaps she put the gleam in my father's eye
that made me nephew. Possible. Probable.
I, no son, although more son to her
than to reluctant mother.

I knew the latest time I saw her would be the last.
I'd not disagree on headlines or weather.
Would comment on her room. Lovely.
Would ask about meals, nurses, others.
Would probe for the story of myself
on a jetty with freshly caught fish
I picked from creels, threw back to
the astonished looks of fishermen. Aged four.
Now the day was beyond her memory, was
even past recollection of the telling.

I tried again. She retold as always:
myself greedy for a suitcase my own size
but led to jumbo trunks too large by
three times or four to my eager eyes.
I stamped my feet. My hands apart
measured the distance of my determination.

She, I, we smiled at our melodrama.
I knew when to exit. How to.
Or thought I did. We kissed.
As I turned to leave I knew
my seventy-nine year old aunt knew
I knew she'd tongue-kissed me.

The Cremation

Without the pinecones
glowing orange
like beetles
& branches
thin & burning
luminous
like scarecrows

the mallee stump
was wood on top
& slow coals
underneath
on greying
dust.

I steamed
a saucepan of water
up the chimney
last night
to put the fire out
& use the mallee again
for today's
fire.

A phonecall dials
my oldest aunt
dead, dying last night –
she who'd often
prayed for
release &
I suppose
for me.

I lift the mallee
onto newspaper, I
gently lay it out
basking
in the sun
like a pumpkin.

Tonight I will
place it on orange coals
before I sleep, knowing
I will find
it powder
fine as mist
in the morning –
ash grey white
in her last years
the colour of
her hair.

Emptying the Ashtrays

I empty his ashtrays. Shift my chair.
Switch on the slow exhaust fan.
He rolls his own & the thick pall
lowers the low ceiling down on me.
He's coughing himself to death &
because of me he's probably coughing more.
We've been through it all before.
He'll always quote some tall chimney
who puffed his lungs to a hundred
or some poor wowser who snuffed it
at forty – lung cancer without a drag.
We both know he's coughing himself to death.
He doesn't find it funny. *I'm* funny.
I'm quick with the slow exhaust.
(We're the quick & the dying.)
I prance around with his ashtrays.
(How the tar sticks to china & glass.)
I threaten to knock a wall out.
Clowning it up. Trying to stay alive.

You Never Know

His first pay didn't amount to a rifle
but nothing could have been more useful
for a young farmhand or a mallee grubber &
if he didn't need it in his barber & bike shops
he always kept it in his truck or ute or car
as the gravel was sealed & his shirts ironed.
If he kept it in a blanket when selling Life
& he no longer needed the rabbits he shot
he was still working the country he'd known
like the back of his hand covered in bees.
You never know, he used to say to himself.
Those who could have asked might have been
at a loss to explain why they didn't ask him
whether there'd been a single hit or miss or
a more & more dressed-up country town or
whether there'd been something else firing
the how, when & where of his last shot
or what must have been his last shot
a good twenty years before the end.

Seventy-nine

A sequence of 11 poems

1
Diabetes
kidney stones
smoke-filled airways
15% circulation in his left leg & then
his head swinging perilously on a
fraying rope of
blood.
After four hours under lights
a length of plastic pipe & valves
installed under the zip of his healing
leaves him unsteady, swaying
above a commode mix of
more than liquid less than solid
tossing his twice used toilet paper
on the carpet, on the table
hitching up his baggy trousers
over baggier underpants
disappointed
he couldn't do it.

2
He knows one of his sons couldn't have
been here to see him yesterday
because that one of his sons
died two years ago.
He knows one of his two remaining sons
couldn't have been wheeled out dead
along the corridor yesterday
because he's coming to
see him today.
Although he doesn't want to know
he knows his wife has left him
if only because she's
not here now.

3
Everything has always been too much for her
& now something is, someone – his ten
or eleven tablets & another cup of tea.
So one District Nurse arrives & nurses
& two Domiciliary Carers arrive & care.
There's an aluminium walker for his walking
lambkins for his bed, his chair, his arsehole
& a plastic urine bottle for his cuppas.
He wants & he wants & he wants &
his wants are the same as his needs.
When he gets what he wants, he wants
what he wants again – because, at his age
he doesn't want to go without. He thinks
he wants to go to bed with his wife.
He does want to go to bed with his wife
for the night at 6.30 pm. Night night.

4
After 45 years his wife hasn't tossed him out.
She's tossed out the man she didn't marry
the man who's no longer the man he was.
He tells her to stay. It's too late.
Ten minutes & she's going, going, gone.
He doesn't mention her until next time.
She becomes his sister, his daughter.
She's not the woman he married. No way.
He can't remember her name or names or
all those places where they lived –
those houses & towns by the river
& the town where they live now.
He grins. Is it Timbuktu?

5
He's in his pyjamas & dressing gown
in front of his favourite television
in Adelaide on a Sunday evening
but he has to take charge of
a motor mower & a box of 78 rpms from
his 83 year old & only surviving sister
who always takes to the wheel of a bus
after Evensong on Sunday evenings &
owns two utes he has to pick up
although she hasn't phoned him &
he wants to but won't phone her
& can't force anyone else to
which proves him right.

6
He doesn't know where he is
in daylight let alone at night.
So I half-sleep in a sleeping bag
near the entrance to his room.
At 3.30 am he's outward bound for
Morgan or Marabel or Saddleworth.
Stopping him, I'm someone I'm not.
Stopped, he drops back on the bed.
Snap. His lifelong friend turns bastard.
I'm Chaddy – whoever Chaddy might have been.
His horse? His dog? His cat? His truck?
Because he's failed to convince me
football will make a man of me &
I'm tired & cold in just my jocks
& sick of shit & senility & not 79
I crank his arm to push him up
to plonk him down on the commode.
His shoulders still swing his axe.
I can't move him unless he moves.
'You hurt me. I'm a human being.'

7
With the rug over his spindly legs
he sits & talks sense or nonsense
irrespective of the nonsense or sense
in the room full of lamps & clocks
he bought for a song & salesmanship
in & around his small country towns.
He wrenches himself out of his chair
& starts walking without his walker
over gravel to the stone farmhouse
in that marginal of marginal country
fenced with fences of dry stone
through paddocks of stones &
wheat never quite as high
as he remembers.

8
At his best, he says
his memory isn't as good
as it used to be.
He apologises.
At his worst, he says
he's going to end it all
he'd rather be dead
he's going mad.
Even with the wherewithal
he'd have only 15% of
the will for his
worst or best.

9
With how much of 100% of
my mind (99%? 98%? 97%?)
will I put up with
how much of 100% of
my body (90%? 80%?
Do I hear 70%?)

10
You'd prefer
a champagne glass full of
bursting crimson petals
going black down
the airways

or
a brain dead stick of
gelignite.

Either/or – so would I.

11
No luck?
Then take on
the shuddering Zs of
black lightning out of what?
out of 99%? 98%? 97% or less of
some cheap old black & white comic
its violet & purple cover torn out of
your first childhood – the electric Zs
flying in from over the hills & far away
when you close your eyes, the Z-dots of
vultures out & about in first light
circling the first chick
to split the atom &
hatch out of
the sun.

Section 5

Henry George

1 Death Notice

Died 1897, editor, author,
journalist, free-trader, single-taxer of land only,
Christian, anti-monopolist, three times mayoral candidate
for New York City,
printer by trade

of his last campaign
his last tract impossible to finish
too many speeches, four a day for five days,
the last the most rambling rave
after arriving late

by his own voice
and choice

of martyrdom.

2 Funeral

The body lay in state
at Grand Central Palace of the People
who filed in the lengthening procession of 100,000
voting in anything but the secret ballot
of his oratory.

Over the casket
a mourner pledged allegiance,
the crowd as congregation
cheering.

Evening. Late-fall.
The open hearse drawn by sixteen draped horses in black.
His bronze bust held aloft Roman style
by the son who shaped
the father's wishes.

'The Marseillaise'.
Chopin's 'Funeral March'.
A white rose dropped from a window bloomed
on the casket by City Hall
over Brooklyn Bridge
to Brooklyn

in the ailing light.

General Patton Returns General MacArthur's Return

Hi Mac. I was kind of expecting you.
I learned to expect the unexpected.
So did you, Mac. That's how we won
& of course when we won, we lost.
The dog house; not the White House.
Yeah, I've fought sword against sword
rifle against rifle, tank against tank
& I've survived every battle, Mac
every battle yielding up survivors.
The victors survive victorious in me.
You said you'd return & so you have.
How come, Mac? You're not even dead.
I can't be *your* reincarnation, can I?
What? You've jumped the queue to say
you're no longer a war-lover. Goddamn!
Don't say you've become an old softie.
Running Japan must have got to you.
An acute case of Mac the Emperor, eh?
No, there's only one enemy – peace.
I love war, Mac. I love soldiers.
You never loved anyone but yourself.
Look at you in your plum satin tie
& your extra-large raccoon coat or
leaning back behind your work desk
in your la-di-da ceremonial kimono
smoking out of your jewelled holder
with your mirror four metres high
behind your chair as if one of you
wouldn't have been enough for the Reds.
Goddamnit General Douglas MacArthur!
If *I'd* been going to nuke the Chinese
do you know who would have been with me?
Attila, Genghis, Hannibal & the Caesars –
all of them staring at a map of China, Mac
staring through the same eyes. Mine. Theirs.

Hemingway's Last Sentence

Women. I don't trust them. Never have. Not since
my mother did my father in & sent me his revolver.
She didn't squeeze the trigger. *He* had to do that.
Can't complain about Mary, though. Fourth time, lucky.
A good shot. A good pair of sea legs. A fine woman.
Even so, it was a trick, a trap. Always is with women.
I don't blame the doctors – professional, even kind.
The Hemingway Institute of Grace Under Pressure –
that's what they could have called the place if
they'd been able to do anything with me, for me.
It wouldn't have done their fund-raising any harm.
Would have been on a par with Budweiser beer & me
across two pages of *Life* magazine. On the piss with Papa.
Piss on with Papa. Pissed with Papa. Piss with Papa.
It's probably too late, now, to flog off a whisky.
How many treatments? Wouldn't know, wouldn't want to.
The doctors lost my memory so I could find it again
(killing the lion because you love the lion, I guess).
Mary says it's coming back. She would, wouldn't she?
I used to do better punch drunk – well, drunk anyway.
Short-term loss for long-term gain. Muck them. Fuck them.
They blew me to bits. There's no long-term. Never was.
Not that it's their fault. There's nothing wrong with me
that a new collection of short stories wouldn't fix.
That's why I've been writing one sentence for weeks.
Still, I'm not going to grizzle. *For Whom the Bell Tolls*
was Castro's manifesto up there in the Sierra Maestra
before his *barbudos* made their move down into Havana.
Even so, peace just isn't the same as war. Just isn't.
Idaho's a fine place. Not all that far from Illinois.
Miss the blue of the Stream, though. Sharks. Marlin.
Call me the old man without the sea. Look old, feel old.
Can't say anything has got to me, though. Everything has.
Here we go. I'm pointing the Boss double barrel up now
thinking of big game. The tension. The excitement.
I've tried fingers, tried toes. Always like detail.
If I angle the barrels up into my mouth now &
squeeze, I'm sure to give Mary & her doctors
something to talk about. *Nada.* Nothing.

Dr Hemingway

$1,000 a day isn't going to be a problem.
So off he goes on safari – buffalo hunting
in the last of the Old American West
Down Under in the Northern Territory.
He knows the buffalo won't be as big
as the massive shaggy pride of Wyoming
but head & neck will still plunge sideways
the last hind leg up in the air, shuddering
after his delicate & well-insured hands
that fondle the liquid crystal pouches of
breasts-to-be, breasts within breasts-to-be
fondle the custom-made high velocity rifle
until he holds it firm among the blowflies
just touching, touching up the trigger
knowing he'll feel tired & let down
as always with the old sad ache of
killing the thing he loves now huge
through the telescopic sight. Pow. Pow.

Camelot & the Greek Widow

I love you, Jack,
she said &
I believed
she believed it.
Why shouldn't I?
The Cold War
was always on the hot plate
Jack, wasn't it?
You were our
noble warrior
reading
your Ian Fleming.
We'd seen the sites
in Cuba –
waiting on missiles
& on your spies
& we'd seen the peasant's boot
come down
hammer & sickle
thumping the UN's
furniture.
You would go anywhere
Jack, you would pay any price –
the price that was
too dear
even for your dynasty.
It's a pity
you didn't live long enough
to lose the war
to bomb them
to not bomb them
back into the Stone Age.
Years later
in the documentaries
the CIA & the FBI & the Mafia
& the odd schizoid crack shot
all conspired or competed
& paid their price
for you, Jack,

but the American Way
returned to
Peace with Honor
& like all other
lessons of politics
reeled off into history
to be forgotten
for Hallowe'en
& a troupe of
marching girls.
Because
we're a bit slow
down here Down Under
I didn't hear
about the film stars
of your domestic policy
on those White House
sofas & afternoons
& your off the record
press briefings
press boastings
on how many
of them
until long after
I wasn't
supposed to be
impressed
or envious
& they're still catting
over you – those
who haven't
overdosed.
I was still
a schoolboy
Jack
but
I loved you
we all loved you then –
competing in debates to prove
just how much we
loved you.

Jacqueline
probably loved you too
Jack, at least the assassin
brought out the
best in her.
I wish
I'd known then
as much as she knew
on that particular
November day
in Dallas.

Hang Loose, Man

Hang loose, man,
said the loose-hanging man
peck-picking away on his guitar
with more guts than the man
& more in his guts
than the man
welcoming home
a loose-hanging Hang loose, man, hang loose,
anything but a conscript of a man
with beer – the slow high. Fast.

The uncool, unloose-hanging
man hadn't peddled a bike through
mine & paddyfields of Cong & spiked bamboo
& hadn't been told
Don't touch by
a Saigon whore too ugly &
too poor to work the bars & hadn't
shot or snorted or just
smoked blinding weed rank
above the tunnels, his heart
pounding like a frog
in a jam tin.

The unhip, uncool, uptight, unloose-hanging man
had only Ho Ho Ho Chi Minhed
when he was a man
& a legend
before he became
a whole city
& died

& now was listening to
footsteps unevenly stressed & disappearing
down the stairs of
some ballad's
Hang loose, man, hang loose

& now was opening windows
on vomit & shampoo.

Alas, Poor Richard

If there'd been errors of judgment
and there'd been some, all made
for America's good – you knew
you could take the opposite view
when jaw faltered once
rehearsed voice phoney as always
the final resignation. He'd
been kicked around so long after
he said no more boots, you can't
believe he's out.

If you'd seen him through school, football, navy,
voted for his first election
watched his newspaper face age
before TV and after, you'd
say he sold out promise.

First knowing him as a crook as he said
I am not a crook, in Disneyland,
hearing him pardoned for offences
he had or may have committed
when you knew he had, you turn
back pages searching for fatal flaws
in newsmagazines of family album:

after-five shadows not looking all American boy;
behind spiderwebbed windows, official car,
he's difficult to see in Caracas;
spadeface uncovering film in pumpkins
could dig and plant too;
though widebrimmed lapels return
he's not quite the man you knew
as lawyer in a stetson, California;
college's football, curly hair,
you'd never recognise him
at 14, artistic boy with cello.

Green cracks concrete path to old clapboard home.
Nothing's eerie, sinister. Braces, hearing aid,
thin white hair, father looks a friendly guy.
You don't see father in son.

Now doctors knife phlebitis. Leg to heart vein ties.
Bloodclots stop from breaking free
to heart, lungs, by blockade. Haiphong.
Cruel to be kind and all that.

The Second Shot

George Reeves missed the first time.
The bullet tunnelled into the ceiling
like a locomotive, his hand
shaking with dope & nerves
or no dope & nerves
or as early as 1959
no hope.
The coroner found the second bullet.

I always thought
George Reeves dived
in his cape & full frontal S
out of some tall building
some newspaper skyscraper
like his alter ego –
the bird, the plane, the Superman
who put the S in USA.

I don't know why
I never saw Clark Kent jump
like the 1,929 jumps in the 1929 crash
to the stockmarket floor I
knew nothing about

like smack
like the DTs
like needing a second bullet to
splash through anything
but steel.

George Reeves always meant something
more than Superman. That's
why I'm sorry
he didn't
dive

& die

once & for all.

Ronald Reagan's Hand

The last time John Wayne denied
he was the last American hero,
he had nothing more in his hand
than Ronald Reagan's hand – *he*
with the whole world in *his* hand.
He had the B-grade movie.
Now he's got the B 1 bomber.
He's got the Cruise missile.
He's got the neutron bomb.
In *Bedtime For Bonzo* he had Bonzo's hand.
He had Bonzo's bananas before Bonzo had them
in a landslide of banana skins
simple as shelling peanuts.
Now he's got the banana republicans
eating out of his hand, like Bonzo.
Most of all, he had my father's hand.
Daddy remembers, even if Ronny doesn't.
So you could say I've almost shaken
Ronald Reagan's hand &
Bonzo's –
me, my father's
my father, Ronald Reagan's &
Reagan, Bonzo's – Bonzo the chimpanzee
in the Oval Office, in a frame,
close to the President's hand.

Eighty-Eight

In Bel Air
at the age of eighty-eight
Ronald Reagan rakes the leaves out of
his heated swimming-pool day after day
hour after hour during the day
& sometimes during the night

his leaves falling into the pool
in winter, spring & summer
as well as in the fall

his leaves all red
the red, the orange
the yellow & the green.

What Chance Has a Girl Got

& that's not the half of it.
Even when I married a professional
(a fine American my fifth husband)
Tonya was still a low class girl.
She was always a low class girl &
then she married that low class boy
even if she did finally get rid of him.
The sacrifices I've made, but do you know what?
I don't think she ever had it in her, the ice dream.
No matter what I said she wouldn't wear white:
she wore red – crimson-red, scarlet-red, any red.
No matter how hard I tried & Lord knows I tried
I just couldn't make her into my ice princess.
If only Nancy Kerrigan had been *my* daughter. *She*
wouldn't have stripped out of a wedding dress
for a video or even a box brownie. No Sirree.
Too much of a Lady to be anything like Tonya
what with her smoking & drinking & some of
those coaches & managers early on.
Let me tell you there's nothing
that girl hasn't done
on ice.

The State of the Union

Billed as the State of the Union Address
to state the state of Bill's union or
preferably the state of Bill's non-union
Bill's State of the Union Address prayed
closed its eyes & thought of Hillary
while looking Saddam Hussein in the lens.
So everyone, but everyone wanted to know
how far the President would have to go
how far the President had already gone.
Had Monica *Lewinskyed* Bill Clinton or
had Bill *Clintoned* Monica Lewinsky?
Instead of going the whole Lewinsky
perhaps Monica just Monicaed Bill –
one & the same as Monicaing Clinton.
Bill mightn't have got any more out of it
if he'd gone the whole Lewinsky but
Monica might have got more out of it
if she'd gone the whole Clinton
Clinton, Clinton, Clinton, Clinton.
Depends on whether or not she thought of
Monicaing as Lewinskying with lipstick.
Anyway, who cares, who cared? Everyone
& no-one once the Navy was on its way
the Lewinsky aircraft carriers carrying
Lewinsky bombers carrying Lewinsky bombs
smart or maybe not-so-smart bombs
some dud bombs, dumb bombs, dumbos
depending on whether they thought with
their Lewinskys or with their Monicas.

One Tree in Ohio

My fellow Americans
call it a wake-up. Yeah, *some* wake-up.
As you will have heard by now, the blackout
was caused by a tree – one tree in Ohio.
Allow me to ask you, my fellow Americans
what could be a greater threat to freedom
than just one tree doing us in, snuffing out
all the bright lights of north-east America
(sure, of course, Canada, sure, Canada too).
If one terrorist can do as much harm as this
then it's our duty to eliminate *all* terrorists.
You bet. We'll chop em down & smoke em up.
From the dogwoods to the cotton woods
from the redwoods to the ponderosa pines
we don't want to see a single sapling
except, of course, for one of each species
to be permanently preserved on reservations
benevolently reserved for our fellow Americans
the Navaho, the Mohawk, the Mohican, the Cherokee
& why the hell, why not call those reservations
the Richard Nixon, Gerald Ford, Ronald Reagan &
hi there, Dad & love to Mum – the George Bush.
Yep, have only to think of fun-loving Americans
trapped in elevators, stopped dead in subways
hanging upside down if not quite inside out
in the amusement parks of this great nation
to see the light of God's Word day & night
oh Lordy Lordy Lordy: Let there be light.
I'm a compassionate conservative, a hard softie
but my compassion has a limit. It won't stretch
to giant bin Ladens, gnarled Saddam Husseins.
Our safety & security lie in pre-emptive strikes
in defoliation, chain-sawing, clear-felling &
tried & trusted & true skill with the axe.
Only a few minutes ago I took a welcome call
from Prime Minister John Howard of Australia &

I know he's ready to assist with his great axemen
from his annual wood chip events (thank you
Co-lin) his annual wood *chop* events. For sure
no stopping until we've imposed the death penalty
on every tree. Ring-barking is too darn slow.
It's no lose. Yep, it's win-win all the way.
We'll put all of our unemployed out to work
& we'll make men of them – even the women
(my apologies, Condoleezza, apologies ma'am).
We'll pull ourselves up by pulling our trees out.
The greenback will go; the economy will be *all* go.
Anyhow, who called it the greenback? Greenies?
Still, I do have one regret. I know in my heart
our children will miss their Christmas trees but
plastic will boom & shine & shimmer once again.
We know that's good for oil & good for America.
Yep, I always put my mouth where my money is.
(Sorry, Co-lin.) As I was saying, this Christmas
the trees will march out of more & more factories
with military precision, always delivered on time.
We promise every child a twinkling Christmas tree.
God bless you, my little ones. Merry Christmas.
Which brings me to bidding you all Good night &
God bless you & God bless a treeless America.

Truman Capote's Quirks

I have to add up numbers, all numbers:
there are some people I never telephone
because their number adds up to unlucky;
ditto, there are hotel rooms I say no to &
no to three cigarette butts in an ashtray.
I won't travel on a plane with two nuns.
They're endless, the things I can't & won't.
I won't begin or end anything on a Friday.
I will not countenance yellow roses – sad
because they're my favourite flowers.

Marilyn Monroe Reads

Miss Monroe's diamond-checked halter neck
holds up, holds in some smooth cleavage.
Her feet are pointing out, slightly
to ensure her legs are close together
so that her knees prop up her fingers
spread out to hold up the Bodley Head
the hardcover she could be posing to read
but does appear to be intent on reading
the latter pages of James Joyce's *Ulysses*
the early pages of Molly Bloom's Yes to Yes.
There's no day or date on this photograph
where Miss Monroe won't upstage Mrs Bloom.

A Slight Acquaintance with John Forbes

When I replied I was teaching
Black Literature
(once Negro &
future Afro-American;
not black ha ha or black peculiar)
he could have acknowledged but wouldn't
the wind in its white sails
before taking the wind
out of mine.

No, I hadn't read
Radical Chic & Mau Mauing the Flak Catchers
but I promised I would &
even keeping the promise
wore the bleeding heart of a
non-Australian liberal
nigger-lover
on its

Then there was the first page of
his atlas of one-liners of
one-up-manship

I almost acquired an acquired taste for

& then well before the last page
something older than sails
bloating across
the Atlantic

something else
I didn't believe in
no matter how highly recommended

Original Sin.

Section 6

Once in a Lifetime, a Perfect Rainbow

On the very same day my wife tossed out
my mother's wedding photograph
with my agreement
but without my
last look

while I was weeding easy to weed soursobs
my fork, as if a divining of water,
struck a weed's greening out of
an empty shell once
a snail.

It was as if all green through pine & grass & vine
had coiled into the one swirling &
swivelled out of not only
the earth but
the sea

& the sky's mist caught the sun in a rainbow
arched so far that my wife & I
had to turn our heads to
find the sky divided
into halves –

once in a lifetime,
a perfect rainbow.

Wedding Anniversary Dream

The slides give way
slowly to speeding grey-blue &
sheer blue down
two sides.

In map-treads
of two mountain rows
fine white sand is cradling,
lying open to sky like half a pipeline
along the range

A woman, lying,
her head at my feet
eases out her first child
slowly, like hour-glass sand sliding
through her fingers
open & relaxed.

I stand still
& she lies not crying or sweating
when the child moves back up into her
easily as the slipping out
& a creature curls slowly
in red petals of
placenta –

the only one
of three creatures
without eyes to see a mauve planet
rolling over the woman's toes –
a wheel turning
in cogs

a circular saw tearing strips of
long low cloud
off its own momentum
before taking off & veering away &
spinning sand into a
net of crimson

only to be fused &
yet still molten – a lava of violet glass
tangled in skeins of
blood

& taking away all shadow & silhouette.

Swiss Strawberry

Tonight against the brown-black leather
I see the Swiss Strawberry Estée Lauder she's
worn for at least two weeks, she says
she even wore it for my father
or at least in his company.
Swiss Strawberry is all it takes – tonight
I want to be the affectionate lover
she no longer wants me to be.
She always called a fuck a fuck.
That's why she married me.
Our dialogue is our own
very much to the point
somewhat repetitive, always stylised
yet capable of Swiss Strawberry variations on
a theme of polished toes
against prick.
I don't want to skite
but I can't say I'm sorry
I was too busy on her birthday
when it can be like this, this.

Mountain Spring

If we'd jumped the creek on stepping stones
& dwindled the path down to a track before
heading up into the outcrops & further up
to the rim rocking to the all rock
berg of a mountain peak

we'd have been searching for the spring
we didn't know we didn't need to find.

We tracked up, straight up
zigzag by steps on ledges, puffing,
resting, downing our water too soon.
Everything was red rock until it
was red rock slab we sprawled on
looking down the view, the rim
around shadowing the iceberg peak.
We eased down the slope.

She didn't take off her top.
I didn't compete with the mountain
or the spring. There was no need.

Neither of us said anything memorable
or even anything we remember.
We remember that.

We cupped our hands in the first pool
our eyes & hands could call a pool.
The iceberg slapped us in the face
& molten glass in the sun
was trickling down the uplands.

Before there was water
there was already water.

The Calling

She calls.
I run out of a pool of
bright desk lamp light into
antique glass light so blue & dusty
it can't light up the cockroach
I'm expected to sink the boot in.
I think I drop something off the sole of
my leather slipper into orange embers
in the black painted fireplace.
I can't see it. Can't see.
There, there, *there,* she screams.
I can't see death or half-death
against black, against fire.
She pulls down the antique & gives me
only a frosted bulb onto whatever
might be left of the cockroach.
There, there, *there,* she screeches.
Ah, shut up.
I can't stand things suffering, she says.
I can't either, I say.

The Slang

One day you arrived home with
Tough titty in your mouth, Tough titty.
She'd known you long enough to know
you weren't Tough titty & T t wasn't you.
She set another place at dinner &
Guess-who's-come-to-dinnered you.
Over the washing up for, yes, three
you started to brood over who'd
come to dinner & spoiled yours
& made you wash the dishes as if
you were washing your mouth out with soap.
Farewell, Tough titty. Tough titty, farewell.

Years later you arrived home to magic.
Something was magic. Something else was magic.
Bloody near everything was magically turned
or turning into what it couldn't be.
It would have been time for Tough titty
if you hadn't been too old for Tough titty
– almost too old for *any* titty. But
the first time you heard her godless Oh my God!
there were Hallelujah choruses full of magic
in your Oh my God! Oh my God!

Stedelijk Museum, Amsterdam, 1978

Now, almost
twenty years later
I remember indelibly
& I even remember
our memories of
spiralling around
the thin strokes
the parallel strokes
bending light into colour
colour into light
the parallels curving
corn, clouds, pinetrees
& spiralling galaxies of leaves
spiralling blue walls
or blue skies
or just blue
until the crows
at the top of
the spiral
crows through everything
crow yellow
crow blue
crow indigo
darker crow
than any postcard
we airmailed. What
I don't remember, though
even when I remember
is that only
one of us
was there.

The Principal's Optimism

She knew she had little hope of
holding onto her old job when she said
The weather looks bad for Sports Day
seeing, early in the morning, she'd
already spoilt the Principal's day.
He tried to clear the clouds away
with a wave of one arm raving
at a small opening of blue.

When it rained all day, even hailed,
she managed to keep out of his way
& learning her lesson, she re-applied
on a clear, crisp, blue Spring day
waiting for Thanks but No thanks.

It would have surprised her if
the new appointee hadn't been younger
a former model, married to a Principal
well qualified (well, almost well)
& bubbling over with optimism.
She wasn't surprise, surprised.

Later, whether she heard the news
on a day humming with early summer or
chilled by a grey-green layer of cloud,
she couldn't say or she wouldn't.
The new appointee had transferred out
for family reasons – although it was said
she'd gone down & down in the dumps
at the sight of smiling suns on windows
the shrieking of Have A Nice Day days
& the heavy to unbearable weight of
all those bright & beautifuls.

Celebration

I will not have any say.
So I say it now for you.
I am not you – celebrate.
I will not be able to say
will I? you are not me.

Every breath I breathe I am
supposed to be breathing in
some of Galileo's last breath
but I am nothing like Galileo
& Galileo would have had only
a theoretical notion of me.

I have said to you many times
I am not you. When then is now
say it, then, for me. Celebrate.
I am not you. I am not you.
I would or will for you.

Parent Interview Night

I'll drive you, she says. To distraction? I ask.
Ha ha ha. It's all very well for you, isn't it.
I'm the one who has to work the long hours.
I'm the one who has to drive through the traffic.
I'm the one who has to help him with his Maths.
But I can't help him with his Maths, I reply
I couldn't even help myself. Well, she says
you could at least help him with *your* subjects.
My subjects? But I'm not going to school anymore.
He's the one who's going to school. We pay enough.
Why can't his teachers start teaching him? Anyway
I didn't want him to go there in the first place.
He's only going there because you like the view.
Here are the teachers' names & subjects, she says.
'Parent Interview Night', eh? Who's who. Who's *whom.*
To interview or to be interviewed: that *is* the question
in the room with a view, in the room with *the* view.
You can't see it at night, she says. Ah! I knew.
All along I knew it was the view & the buildings.
I'm going to get the keys. All you've got to do
is find the right teacher, look, listen & learn.
Yes, but I finished learning when I left school.
For Christ's sake, open the gate. We'll be late.
You'll go down in the next census as a lapsed atheist.
Remember, just say Hello & be friendly. That's all.
I can't just say Hello. I'll have to say Good evening.
Good evening, Mrs English. Good evening, Mrs Science.
Good evening, Mrs Maths. Good evening, Mr History.
Good evening. Good evening. Thank you. Good night.
What grade do you reckon they'll give me?
I'll be back in the car park by 9.15pm.

Mrs English is first. Just as well. If she were last
I'd know it was nearly time for school to be out.
I'd relax, lounging in the chair, speculating on
which year Mrs English had first heard English – was
it the year I gained my First Class (Hons.) English?
& just by the way, say, ask almost lackadaisically
whether Mrs English knew how many columns I took up

in the second edition of Wilde, Hooton & Andrews'
Oxford Companion to Australian Literature, The.
Well, she would have been new to the school &
probably still getting used to the view out of
the window of the room with a view, *the* view.
I know I only have to say Hello & listen & so
I say Good evening & listen to Mrs Science who's
careful not to balance an equation of father & son.
She'll take out of the computer what she puts in
eventually, but not for Parent Interview Night.
Suits me. Mrs Maths is the next one to take care
not to say anything like like father, like son.
Father should know that son should know she offers
extra classes by extra special appointment because
you know, they don't want their mates to know. No.
I like the old girl. A brick, if not a good old stick.
Passing Science & Maths for the first time ever
I sense I'm nearly there, at least I'm on my way
to some heavy petting in the car park at 9.15pm.
After all, I'm supposed to be going back to school.
When Mr History says History, I almost say PhD.
To Mr History's Of course it *is* some time ago
I can't help adding it wouldn't surprise me
if the whole class found History totally remote.
Not a Great Moment of History for him – or me.
Mr History can't believe History's repeating itself.
He has ended up with another end-of-History man
the only History Dad knows ending History forever.
How on earth can I recover without my PhD – or *with?*
I try watching *Foreign Correspondent* with my son.
I try Ok Tedi, Bougainville, Papua New Guinea.
I throw in Sir Julius Chan as *he* throws in the towel.
It mightn't be a Great Moment of History yet
but it might be when it's no longer on the news.
Mr History sees there's still hope for me & history.
He'll connect the PNG Army with Napoleon Bonaparte.
Knowing me, my son foresees his hard-earned As
toppling to Bs like the heads of Kings & Queens.

Fine-Tuning

After twenty-seven years of it
it's not as if your life's over
but you'd think common sense
would tell you you've
pressed every button &
pulled every knob
even if you haven't climbed every mountain.
So you're not shocked (& you
wouldn't let on if you were)
you're surprised when she informs you
your mouth around her nipples is okay, not bad
but what she really likes is a
twiddling of the very two-at-a-time tips
& it's almost as if she's going
to give you a demonstration
before you get the message
that your marriage is
basically sound –
just in need of
fine-tuning.

Sex for the over 50s

We've finally got around to it
not sex, not sex at over fifty
but sex in the bed we sleep in.
Not only are we sleeping together
but now we're sleeping together
too. If sex for way, way under 50s
was a hard mattress on a wooden base
I aged & aged & aged in my first water bed
& every bed became just another water bed
so that every floppy moment had to be
lived in an aching twilight of nostalgia for
cheap wooden second-rate second-hand furniture.
Good sex can have a bad effect on your sex life.
Let's go to floor or to ground is no substitute for
anything firm on a firm wooden bed base. So
what's got into us? Is it the water?
Is it what's *in* the water?
I've quite lost my fear of quicksand
& running up stairs without rising any steps.
With a little help from brass bed ends
we're virtually into yoga by 3 am 4 am.
We don't need videos. We don't need
anyone else on the phone or in the bed.
There's nothing we don't seem to be
able to do for ourselves. Even so
about noon it comes on – the half-memory
as half-dream, half-hallucination.
We wouldn't. We couldn't have.
We didn't, did we?

Dirty Talk

You have to believe in what words can do
to do this. She does. I do. We do. There's

something about how we've got it off
to get us off that stops me from asking

Did you go on like this before we met?
Have I always gone on like this with you?

I don't think we started when we started.
I would have been first but not by much.

When we don't, we don't give it a thought;
when we do, we can't think of anything else.

Long-Suffering

I'm long-suffering
she says & she says
she's long-suffering
a few hours later &
only a few minutes
after that she says
she's long-suffering
& then after only
a minute or two
she says it again:
I'm long-suffering &
then again & again:
I'm long-suffering
I'm long-suffering &
I'm long-suffering too.

The Dresses

It wasn't as if we had to have costumes
but Carol & I seemed to have lost our clothes –
at least those we wore when we wore clothes.
So Carol was more than pleased to fit into
a short summery-green cotton dress she'd
worn as a teenager, almost as a virgin.
All the know-all men she knew had wished her
Happy International Women's Year all too often &
so she'd undress exactly as she'd dressed, she said
laughing, No, I'm *not* going to strip for you.
Still, she dressed me up in a silk Chinese jacket
a pale pink tracery threaded through baby blue
& wasn't she one turned-on wardrobe mistress.
She even said she was – I cannot tell a lie.
Now, anyone not Chinese in a Chinese jacket
would be working in Tourism & Hospitality
but not way back then in The Good Old Days.
Bright young things just out of the 60s, we
thought we were quite, well, quite quite.

I invite my wife, Diane, to my stage production.
To my amazement & consternation, she accepts.
I have to warn her I'll be wearing a dress
but somehow I don't quite manage to warn her
I'll be wearing her black & red wedding dress
I've unrolled out of a green garbage bag
hidden away in the bottom of her wardrobe.
I mean I wouldn't want to appear on stage
only in my wig, my boa, my jocks & lipstick.
The show must go on & the show does go on &
after the show, Diane & her best friend, Helen,
invite me for a well-deserved supper.
I go. They simply adored the show.

Every time I'm going to do a new show, now
I have to come up with a new argument for
staging myself, upstaging myself all over again
in my wedding dress, my wife's wedding dress.
I don't know when I've felt more at ease.

Which can't help but remind me of Peter. Now Peter
was a man's man if ever there was one – a man
as homophobic as it's possible to be phobic – Peter
who kept buying me lunch & looking me over, apparently,
Peter who said he found something feminine there
here, I mean & I wasn't even wearing a dress.

If the His & Hers wedding dress ever gets lost or
disappears in a puff or two of black & red smoke
it has been said that Josephine has said that
she, well, she has rows & rows of dresses
she'd just love to fit me into.

Section 7

The Greening of Queen Victoria

Sceptre in hand, she
was presiding over the sceptred isle
(the traffic island)
dividing (& ruling) the bitumen into channels
as I stepped off the footpath
onto the hot molten waves she ruled
Queen Victoria looking up at the clocktower
propping up the scaffolding
propping up the tower

& those long strips of hessian patched together
(from Hong Kong or an India once of the Empress?)
down all sides of the tower
& capped at the top
indisputably
a condom
100 metres high.

Stepping up onto the other curb I looked
up & around to where she looked up,
half expecting to see the nineteenth century
blush & saw instead her face green
with old bronze green &
green with envy.

On the authority of some petty official,
workmen, a few days later,
cut the clockface out of hessian
so that Queen Victoria could count
the minutes of the hour &
the days of the month.

The Grapes

Stand under the trellis
in late afternoon. Leaves
won't keep the sun out of
trailing green bubbles of grape.
Look up through this bunch
swollen with rain
around a pale green sun
in each one
revolving around the seed.
Birds puncture the topmost blooms
crystallising yellow, brown, full of sugar.
Bees stretch open the splits, sucking,
hollowing out the grape sacs
into small caves of succulent flesh
now wrapped in flapping skins, fermenting.

Look up again, look at the sun
through these grapes. You'll taste wine.
The cool rim of glass touching your lips
is the first breeze of the last of
summer. Taste it on your skin.

The Crystals

On an old family map
the far, stony paddocks
slope up to outcrops of rock
shooting yucca blooming
once a year alive & yellow
out of fine bending needles green
& cutting me like razorblades
when I grab the wrong way
to avoid a spider
on its trapeze
swinging into my face.
Webs are everywhere.
I cobweb as I go
with a dead yucca.

Above the trees now
the bare sun's on my back
but there's a spar of
light in my eyes
as I pick one
out of the gravel
as if it were a mushroom –

a quartz crystal
a clear six-sided sword
grown through millions of years
in a bed of delicate swords
bristling, broken off, buried
& panned by the sun

a talisman
& many more in my
cache, my loot, my hoard –

all worthless.

I find them lying like ingots
or stuck at odd angles
out of gravel
like bobbins
catching & threading
the sun.

I scour & scrape off
their green-black & I ache
as they come up
geometry
in my hands.

When it rains it rains
crystals –
always upwards.

A Back Full of Bones

You let the fire die
down & crumble the orange
with one raw leather glove
& a tap of your tongs.
You strip to your jocks
& run outdoors into the cold
you belt away from your body
with your sledgehammer thudding down
on concrete, concrete that cracks
through lead & wooden handle
like electric shocks
up your arms &
strapped around
your back.

A few hunks & mostly gravel now. Inside
you drop a long light twist of mallee
onto the greying orange embers &
cool down while the flames
play through wooden holes
with gas hissing out of
this instrument without a name
almost a cry of pain.

Tomorrow &
outside cold again & you
lift the sledgehammer with bare hands
& your bones are filled with cold sweet fire
& your fingers are filled
& your back is filled
with bones.

Wild Hops

Red,
red turning
the red ranges salmon, they

spread like thistles opening into sweetpeas,
their red sloping up the uplands &
climbing still further up
cliffs of quartz –

seeds,
seeds sewn into saddles
& sown out of worn-out saddles
the Afghan camel drivers used to lead the way

towards
the red future
cast & fallen on stony ground,
edge & cranny & narrowing ledge
up there on the high outcrops
every winter come spring

red,
red turning
the red ranges salmon.

Sting-ray, Whyalla

Under iron circles still turning
search-lights on the invisible enemy –
under concrete bunkers blocked into the hill
like Moroccan postcards of Mediterranean sun
framing the sea into long horizontals from shadow
where paint leaves blood on the concrete
& blood leaves a message from
no-one to no-one
but
a helicopter pilot over
an ingenious DROP DEAD
on the roof –

the cry goes out.

Along the jetty, through rails,
the boys are gloating over
a sting-ray, hooked. A sting-ray gaffed
with cross-gaffs (one in one breathing-hole).
They're working it around the pylons.
They're clearing the decks. They're
wearing their gloves, their knives.
It's making their day –

this sea-swelling black on blue sea-kite
no longer flying black through blue
but floating, now, on ripple ribs,
tail limp, then thrashing
as a gloved arm disarms it –
the spike. The boy lifts up the ray by
the hand-holds of breathing-holes
as if holding the handles of a bicycle
to cut the hook out of
the white underside of black &
then turns it over again
like flipping a flounder on a plate
with a kind of etiquette

before letting it slip back
like a black umbrella opening & closing
then flapping, slowly flapping
back into blue –

two metres of wing
slowly flapping.

The Poppies

We're first person singulars
snipped & burned into plurals of
red-pink, red-orange, gold-saffron.
We're solar-powered openings to
pollen-rings on hair triggers
firing on hairy green stems.
We're flare & flounce & flair.
We pop out of our skins
permanently creased & crinkled
insideout umbrellas insideout.
We don't wilt or shrivel.
First person singulars &
first person plurals, we
flake off petal by petal.

Unopened Poppies

Separate the unopened poppy buds
from the flouncing poppies
& arrange them in a vase.
Instant Giacometti. Only olive.
Hairy earmuffs on hairy stems or
tiny microphones on twisted wire
they could be victims of
radiation or liquid nitrogen,
could be the shape of a virus
enlarged a million times or
walking sticks to help gnomes
waiting for elective surgery

until a muff-full or a mike-full
or a bud-full of crushed petals
opens with a motherhood statement
in orange or saffron or pink.

A Rope-Trick

7 am. A rope-trick of cloud
twisted tight on the hills, twisting loose
into a pale blue towards a 10 am sun
as if the petals of a foxglove
were falling, falling upwards;
a waterspout with a neat hem
sewn into the windward &
fraying away downwind;
the tailbone of some dinosaur
that never walked the earth,
so delicately made out of feathers –
cream in this early sun &
whiter than ice before 8 am.

One Jacaranda

Leaving the light to the light
it would take mountains to turn your sun
green. Mountains. Tropics.

One jacaranda turns your sun mauve.
You feel you could hold this one tree
as a torch down a coal mine or
carry the mauve away from the sun
as a gift to the edge of
wherever
& still know where
you & your luminous mauve
would be going –

changing the colour of

the light.

The Speed of Violet

There will be
violet & yellow irises.
Now there's a
slim green plait of stem
shooting a tip of
dye violet
pure as a minute
or an hour
or the time it takes
the first petal to flounce
to stop arrowing up
an invisible target
violet
about to burst
at the speed of light.

The Cent Outside the State Bank

By the time you've bent down to
pick up the cent on the footpath outside
the main entrance to the bevel-edged
sword of the State Bank, you know
you'll go through with it. So
before you begin to bend –
before you begin to think of
bending or beginning to bend –
you know everything doesn't depend
on whether or not you bend
but a government could
depend on it & the
idea of an empire.

The Laundries

Today I launder.
Yesterday I laundered.
I have been laundering.
I've gone to the dogs to launder –
the trots, the casino, the racetrack.
I've registered whole companies
whole holding companies
just to wash out the filth.
No way I want to be caught
off balance, off balance-sheet
or off, just plain off.
So now I launder in laundries
a chain of coin laundries. Mine.
They're off off balance-sheet.
So obvious no-one would look.

Adelaide & Ayrton Senna

Adelaide couldn't find a way to mourn Adelaide
couldn't lay a wreath or two on the State Bank
empty shops, empty storeys, empty buildings;
couldn't lay a lei on 333 Collins Street
that part of Adelaide apart from Adelaide.
Adelaide couldn't find a way to mourn Adelaide's
Grand Prix still roaring endlessly around & around
a lake circuit in another city, another State.

Now Adelaide has found a way to mourn Adelaide.
Adelaide sprays wreaths & flowers & petals &
graffiti on the scorched earth of Adelaide
& insists on calling it Ayrton Senna.

Death by 'Tiser

Enough is. That's it. You're cancelling.
You're awake earlier than early, waiting
for the non-thump of your non-newspaper
when, an hour later, it lobs & lands.
You give your newsagent a week's grace.
Again you wait for nothing to lob & land.
It does. Over the fence, daily by day.
You phone the answering machine once, twice
but the machine won't phone you twice, once.
You write once again, once again polite.
There's no way you're going to pay any more
but you stop unwrapping them on principle.
A few weeks later & they're still lying
higgledy-piggledy around your front yard
lying like long turds dropped by large dogs
bingeing on bones. A few months later &
lo & behold! you're ankle-deep in *'Tiser.*
If you throw them back, you're sure to
smash wheels into fatal wheels or become
the what-not-to-do of Neighbourhood Watch.
So you find you're in deep, knee-deep in *'Tiser.*
Your wife has gone; your son is going to go.
Cancelling hasn't cancelled the day by dailies.
Re-cancelling won't. They just keep on coming:
the thinning cylinders & Saturday's thumper.
Then Eureka! Saturday after Saturday, you
angle & average Saturday's throwing arm
over your fence out of the delivery van.
Then, one Saturday, an hour before sunrise,
you mount the bone-yard of your front yard
you stand on top of your own mass grave
full frontally at full *'Tiser* angle &
you wait & wait & wait & wait &

The Wheelbarrows

Lined up outside the hardware store
they'd been gay for years
these plain metal wheelbarrows
closely fitting into one another
back to front front to back back to front
the manager putting into practice
the domino theory of marketing
or perhaps just short of space
or a closet sculptor.

Now some new theory of marketing
hangs them along the wire fence & daily
takes them down from their crosswire
to save the world from a graffiti of
nightly sex & politics if not religion
these plain concaves of barrows
impaled on a wheel & two handles
these radar, these satellite dishes
filled with emptiness.

The Footpaths

I cannot be the only walker walking.
I know there will be shoppers shopping &
even more shopping in shopping centres.
I have sometimes been there, been one.
I know that houses house the living but I
have never seen the living on the television of
their front windows through blinds & curtains.
if I approached one of those bright windows
if I approached one of those who must be there
I would see only myself walking towards me.
Perhaps they are all behind their wheels on wheels.
I think they think their wheels are more than wheels.
Walking along these paver, concrete & bitumen footpaths
though, I have neither passed nor overtaken anyone.
No-one walks these footpaths. No-one at all.

The Tantrum

The video hire shop requires a renewal
right now, late this Friday afternoon.
If only it weren't too late for If only.
I ask for the Manager. He's out. Always.
Who's next in the pecking order? I ask
sorry to see this three women video game.
It might be harder but easier with men.
Formally I introduce myself & my son.
As if I need to prove paternity
I unfold my ageing Birth Certificate
slam down my investment account &
then my fat hundred cheque chequebook.
That should be enough, I fume, I shake.
I couldn't even take out a membership
last time without a driver's licence.
I don't have a driver's licence &
I don't have a driver's licence
because I don't drive a car &
I don't drive a car because
I don't want to drive a car.
(I can't drive a car, I don't say.)
Calm down, says my son. His mate disappears.
I'm astonishing myself. I'm acting
but the act is no act I'm acting.
I'm staging my own tantrum in Unley.
I know how Hitler did it in Nuremberg.
It's in your wife's name, she says
but it'll be okay. I've won, I think.
Unfortunately that game has now gone.
If ever there were a time for me to go
over the counter, over the top, it'd be now
but I'm speechless. A gutless wonder.
My son's mate reappears. My son.
They'll settle for some other video game
perhaps for *any* other video game.
I move back. While I'm waiting
I can only hope for a hold-up.
She's sorry about all this, she says
but would I like a sweet or a soft drink?

About the Other Day

Oh! Good. I wasn't sure you'd be here.
Look, I'm not sure I should be asking.
I probably shouldn't be but I'm here
anyway. So may as well. Here we go.
About the other day, I know you had to
go – well, I found out you had to go
when you spoke up & told me so & I'm
very glad you did. Of course I am.
I know I'm always likely to rabbit on.
I hope I didn't *run* out of your room
but once I got the message loud & clear
the last thing I wanted to do was stay
while endlessly on the verge of leaving.
By the time I was on my way out, well
in the short time I had to think
before I was on my way out the door
& all the time I've had since then
I got to wondering whether or not
there might have been something else
I'd done or said, you know, earlier.
Nothing definite, nothing specific
but perhaps you *didn't* have to go.
No? There wasn't anything else?
Perhaps you're just not letting on.
No? Well, I'm pleased to hear that.
I'm really pleased to hear that.

Section 8

On the Menu

I'll eat anything. I mean it.
But don't say you won't
have lunch with me.
I won't drink the soup.
I'll even try your wine
in case someone's trying
to poison you – or us.

Still, I warn you I've
eaten an evolution of white bait
oysters, prawns in their shells
baby octopuses, squid, shark.
I'd eat whale steak. (Harpoon, please.)
I've done in a buffalo.
I'm only sorry I'm too late
for dinosaur, tyrannosaurus.
I've had quail, pigeon, pheasant.
I've downed eel, frogs' legs.
I adore bringing snails
out of their shells.
I'd try snake – goanna
if snake's off the menu.
Chocolate ants – no worries.

Eat or be eaten. Be eaten or eat.
Not to say dog eat dog. If you
want to eat me before I eat you
make sure you can use your tongue.

Save the Krill

Down in the fjord
the whale circles upwards
unwinding its air hose, spiralling
up & up going around & around
until the bubbles boil in a wreath
& the krill go down the hatch
caught in the air's net
& scooped like coal
from an opencut.

The whale you save
has a brain almost big enough
to invent a gas oven.

Save the whale &
save the killer –
not the krill.

Other Life

It will not be love at first sight.
We will kill – for it will be
different from ourselves.

Our medicos will plunder its dead
for new life valves to replace
our spare-part replacements.

Our missionaries will bring it back alive
in earthsuits & try to teach it so
it will crusade among its own –

too alien to be earthling
& too human not to be
inhuman.

We will send it off to asteroid wastelands
cracking its planets open like eggs
for precious yokes of new ores.

When it tries to land in our cities
like a true colonial of empire, we
will round it up in helicopters

& stamp stamp stamp it
when we cannot stamp it out
& we will shut it up

& shunt it in long skytrains
to dead moon reservations
where it will nag & gnaw –

dead moons we will claim as our own moons
& then give back – as if they
are ours to bestow.

New Year Resolution

This year I sincerely & solemnly resolve not
to underestimate the intelligence of brontosaurs.
I'm not deterred by late last year's theory of
the big, alive & eggless births of baby brontos.
I know Christmas Day dawned on Emeritus Professor X
measuring the pelvic outlet size of a female bronto
to make sure it's big enough to hold his theory.
I concede the appeal of Mummy brontos protecting
their babies from bronto-bashing Daddy brontos &
other saurs you *won't* find in Roget's *Thesaurus.*
Just after Christmas it's truly reassuring to know
brontosaurs weren't slow-witted, egg-laying & leaving
reptiles with the morbid morbidity rates unearthed in
the fossil graveyards or hatching mortuaries of
other saurs you *will* find in Roget's *Thesuarus.* But.

The last two brontos had a bit of fun getting
all their eggs together in the one basket &
then, with a swish of their marvellous tails,
they shredded all the evidence. The eggs. See?
Don't underestimate the intelligence of brontosaurs.
They decided to call it a day. Call it an Age.
There was always a fear of meteorites or
worse still, sure as eggs, the human race.

Hurting

Now, all hurt is hurting.
A hurt, any hurt, all hurt is hurting.
When I used to hurt you, you were hurt;
now when I hurt you, you are hurting.
When you used to hurt me, I was hurt;
now when you hurt me, I am hurting.
Death (or birth) can stop the hurt
but nothing can stop the hurting.

What we will take with us into the sun
if there is anything left of us to take
is our hurting & our knowing
X million dinosaurs were hurting
from a plentiful lack of fodder

our hurting & our not knowing
whether the universe is hurting
(as it tears itself inside out)
anything or anyone but us.

Section 9

Leonardo da Vinci Visits Australia

There with Leonardo
galloping over the Tuscan hills away
from anonymous letters pointing at heresy &
the trial adjourned when one of
the accused announces his
line with his name's
Medici

there on straw yellow grass
with da Vinci flat on his back re-creating
the wings of flight & creating
the wings of
angels

there with Leonardo
down in cellars of the dead
snipping & slitting & probing & prising open the corpse of
an old man only minutes before contented with what
was left of his lot ripe & sweet & beautiful
& clean the cutters mapping a geometry of
veins & organs & muscles & vertebrae
in search of ripeness
or peace

there in Lombardy where mist forms the
immediate distance of water rippling through pines
as if water were the wind far away tipping
the same pines & further away yet
the mist stitching them
as shadows into
a tapestry

there with Lodovico
Leonardo's patron prince conquering
his last state with bronze cannons – bronze
never used for the twenty-three foot horse
never more than da Vinci's model &
hundreds of sketches &
a few footnotes

gone with extravaganza of
fire & steam & wooden wheels interlocking
spectaculars there for the Medici lover of magic
& to hell with Copernicus &
up & telescoping
Galileo.

Waiting here for Leonardo to die
an apocryphal death in the arms of the French King
I wonder what difference it would have made if the first
hand to circumnavigate Australia by sail
or for that matter by submarine
had been the hand that sliced
the old man's frontal lobe
like ripe pawpaw

the left hand of Leonardo
da Vinci.

The Seacoalmen

Out of their huts and into the fog, their
double torches before light's breaking
so they can back their trucks
into their not quite breakers, they
shovel from the just dawn's creaming
no mullet but small waves full of coal,
the sea coal men compete crew against crew
for the evening's wash into mud and sand.
Salt eats away two new trucks per year.
Sometimes they ram each other, slam
truckdoors open and shut, shove, hassle,
occasionally hit a member of an opposing crew.
The seacoal men sell their coal by bagfulls,
keeping only enough to keep themselves in embers
and money down for their women, holding
them to themselves against the cold, so cold
it almost sears them black like frostbite.
Every six months they save enough money
to buy another truck to skid into fog,
sea, dawn, cold, wet cold, the seacoalmen.

Seeing is Believing

Like wrapping
you wrap yourself
around some invisible holy maypole
as you go up & up
& around & around
the spiral
staircase

towards

the dome
& the dome's
spire.

Bowing
your head
you bob through a narrow door
& you're a handrail away
from death's
plunge
onto the marble floor
before the altar.

You jut out at 100 metres high
on a flimsy wooden walkway
circling the base of
the dome
above.

You grope for
the nearest support &
you climb up three wooden tiers
to reach the one
nearest the wall

only to hear
a loud whispering
from mother to child
from a semi-circle away &
testing testing testing
900 year old
acoustics.

You scaredy cat,
you don't want to think
about what's under you
but, there, under you
there are white & golden angels flying
on trapezes over the high wire
through a brilliant glass mosaic
like pages torn out of
illuminated manuscripts.

By the EXIT
a priest watches over you
& reads a book
which is not
THE BIBLE
but still serves his purpose –
staving off boredom
between the suicide
threats.

You move
hesitantly
towards the EXIT
& EXIT
always keeping
some part of your body
against the wall

relieved now
as you unwind yourself
back down the staircase
that you did not confess
what could have been

your first
pang of religion

to the young priest
who would have assured you
it was just your
fear of heights.

A Secondhand Freudian Interpretation of Hal Colebatch's Discovery of a Marxist Lavatory Under St Paul's

There will be no more epiphanies in St Paul's
(at least not for the male Paulines).
Once again the Greater London Council
has taken unilateral action against
private property, private privacy, private parts.
The underground lavatory at St Paul's
is no accident of glass & porcelain.
A sub-committee of planners planned it.
A sub-committee of accountants accounted for it.
A too too solid solidarity of workers worked
kilns & furnaces & factories & brickyards
to sit this comrade in his (yes, his)
cloth cap & glass-fronted booth
only to look down a lineup of
an instant collective of
a proletariat of
men urinating in a tiled room to
a musak of 'The Red Flag' flying

all, all urinating but Prince Hal
straining, struggling desperately to think of
the Berlin Wall, the Great Wall of China
& the outer walls of the Kremlin

while ascending into the epiphanies of the font above
& the epiphanies above the font above.

The Stonehenge Poem

Every poem should be a Stonehenge poem.
The chalkplain was bare & grey every winter
until landscaped with nineteenth century trees.
Stonehenge is what is left of stone, of blue stone
after quarrying, after souveniring & of brown stone
after graffiti on stone & carved into stone. Dig
into the burial mounds piled into grassy pyramids
& cremation will tell you a story of fire.
New aerial photographs will circle you
around the ditch & central mound full of
bones charred at regular intervals
around the now broken circle of stone
& the inner horseshoe of stone. Put
your back to the highest monolith &
your eyes will be longing for that one light –
the year's longest day when the fire
that must be death marks the turning of
another year. The heel stone polishes
the sun into facets of lightgems & the
year moves in a quarter circle of dawns
moons, tides & eclipses like a clockwork
of stone fitting stone into stone. Chant
in Stonehenge. Blast Rock 'n' Roll. Dance.
Expose no more than one pregnant woman to the sun
once a year & dare to call it magic & no more.
There are no stepping stones to Stonehenge stone.
There are other ways of dressing stone but the
weight of them doesn't weigh on Stonehenge stone.
Doesn't paint or fresco or mosaic these slabs
memory banking their own movement many times
more than anyone has gone around the sun.
Every poem should be its own Stonehenge.

One Kind of Snow

One kind of snow is very light snow
like dandruff on black leather shoulders.
There's snow that bites down on even teeth
out of narrow gauge corrugated iron. Snow
that curves off and under big gauge iron roofing
like the bones of some enormous whale. There's
snow that clears and cones down into long ice or
melts on tile roofs as if tiles were ice. There's
snow sliding down high angles, folding, wrinkling
around gables and chimneys like rolls of dough
baking away in gutterings of a slow sun's oven.

So, twinkle down, silver snow and ice.
I don't care. I know there is no silver.
I don't care whether your snow is icing
or your icing, snow.

Keep your fit. Your outfit. Your synthetic snow.

Keep your ace, your ice of diamonds.

There is only one kind of snow.

The Nineteenth Century

To explore
the maritime & military history of
Marc-Joseph Marion Dufresne's giant tortoise
place time in places – not in the nineteenth century
as if the nineteenth century were a place
but under the North's green & lilac lights
& over the South's million sunrises
waddling upsidedown over ice.

Was Marion's tortoise
half-old or half-young in 1768
when shipped from the Seychelles to Mauritius?
Under the influence of the eighteenth century
it kept the whole of the nineteenth century
under its shell into the twentieth century
half a mine at sea, a pill-box on land
falling off a wall in the last year of
The War to End All Wars
causing World War 2.

Snow Over Alsace-Lorraine

Here where snow is over Alsace-Lorraine
the Cross of Lorraine stands over Alsace.
Snow is along the two cross bars, snow
that is over roads opening up
with red snowploughs sliding by.
I ride a warm bus up the cone
slopes coning far too steep for
anything but reflex hand to hand
in land now one country, now another.
Snow is over Alsace-Lorraine where those
with long memories speak in two
tongues – neither of them mine.

Snow purifies into stalactites of ice
like some huge pipe instrument dripping strings.
Hand to hand an icicle is a bayonet. Close
together, they knit into shawls of ice –
no warmth against first or last snow
overnight and fighting land to land.
Following the road following the stream
I stare at small icicles above the water
lining up in rows along roots and low branches.
French or German icicles with heavy smoke
over them from the factories of Lorraine
unfold around the grey-green stream –
icicles evenly side by side set
like bullets for machineguns.

Joan of Arc

The coals
alive & orange
silhouette
the shape of
mallee –
a suit of
armour
a woman's
torso
a woman's
suit of armour
like heavy placenta
heaved up against
the light.

When I walked
through the long
strings of
stone &
the peacock
& turkey gobbler
blue of
Notre Dame
it was a
bad day
for saints
Joan.

There was
only one
candle
writhing
for you &
we know why
that's always
there.

I should have
bought & lit
another candle
from the candle
for you
Joan.

You're black
silhouette
you come back
with the flames
to curse me
Joan
Joan of Arc
like the witch
like the woman
they always
said you were
inside the
man.

I don't
believe them, Joan.
I see only
torso
armour
& placenta –
no placenta.
I wish I
could flame
this fire
for you
higher than
any candle
Joan
without
roasting you
alive –

again.

Swimming at Lucerne

Up the mountain by cable car.
Up through cloud marooning a low peak
as if it were an island in a lake
above Lake Lucerne. I lean on &
around zigzag corners, tobogganing
my heels in for left or right turns
through sky made of day old snow.

Tourist, I do everything tourists do;
only one better, this time. I swim
through green water. Under glass.
Along one lane & back I'm free of buses
taxis, planes, cable cars, even toboggans.
Breast stroke without bubbles or splashing
moves me through melting white sky down
from mountains like icebergs – the softest
water I've opened up with my fingers & arms
& muscles as I glide through like a lover
up & down the green lane without tiring.

The banks, of course, are awash with blood.

Hard Light

The way I learned it, sailors were Dutchmen.
One must have died up there in the North-West
nearer than he knew to a treasure of diamonds
or perhaps it was just maps, Empire, territory.
Anyway this Dutch Captain nailed something
he wanted to nail *to* something
(probably a tree if he could find one).
I don't remember what was worked on it
but what it *was* comes back to me
now like a slice of moon
like debris from outerspace

a pewter dish

a plate of New Holland light

softer on the English Eastern seaboard
greener than thick English green
in oils;
washed-out as silhouette through mist
in watercolours;
blurred as shadows drawn
in black & white

although, for a while, the hard life.

Last night I landed from London too late
for a connecting flight & the airline
paid the motel bill duplicate of
London's – except for
thick steak on the plate
for breakfast.

Now I split the curtains
& look out through thick glass
on sun over dry summer paddocks –
grey-brown-white-silver alloy of
lethal tin & lead pewter

I've never seen before

the soft life, the hard light.

The Museum of Atheism

The Museum of Atheism
can't be a cathedral emptied by decree of
the opiate of the people,
guides like angels gloating over
the body of a saint –
St Dummy
stuffed with straw.

The Museum of Atheism
can't be a mosque without Muslims
without tanks & rocket launchers &
ammo stacked up the minarets
going off like sky rockets
high on prayer &
nitroglycerine.

The Museum of Atheism
would be the last candle snuff of
air at the very tip of the
candle snuffer of a
Buddhist temple
if nothing could he pointed to
sans Buddha *sans* Buddhas
sans everything.

Under the Floorboards

Renovating, creaking up floorboards
flipping through an old newsmagazine
at last, at last, I think I have. Turning
THE WORLD to a full-stop, I know I have
found where I'll always want to be
as long as I don't have to be there:
Albania on the 17th of November 1986.
Two white horses pull the kitchen windows of
the windscreen-wiperless windscreens of
what looks like a home-made truck –
a coach & horses without the coach.
The caption is only a Cold War caption: if
ploughs are pulled by yoked teams of women
surely there would be photographs of
ploughs pulled by teams of yoked women.
Even the facts that are facts don't or
can't speak for themselves: Albania
neither East nor West of anywhere &
rising in thousands of concrete bunkers
visored with the narrow gun slits of
Ned Kellys neither rich nor poor
with nothing borrowed, nothing owed;
churches, mosques & synagogues – museums
easily turned into museums (bless them);
& out of a population of three million
only a few hundred cars (oh! sweet air).

Accident, the Urals

Impossible
but results came out radioactive
the effects of & effects on the active.

Impossible
but people were moved on & moved out
& ordered to remain in their cars driving through.

Impossible
but all buildings scorched the scorched earth
so no-one could retrieve irretrievable belongings.

Impossible
but all farms are ghostfarms of chimneys
& towns are laid to rest under layers of asphalt.

Impossible
but victims die in separate wings
parts of yet apart from hospital death & dying.

Impossible
cancer impossible impotence (impossible vodka)
& faces red with overdose like eczema (yes, impossible vodka).

Impossible
for enough plutonium to waste the earth
& enough rain to leach down through soil & plutonium

impossible yes impossible
for earth to boil & steam & bubble &
croak open a man & woman-made volcano of mud poison

impossible yes impossible
death impossible half-life impossible half-death
impossible death impossible death impossible death impossible birth.

Filmclip

I saw the officer raise his pistol &
fire. Saw the soldier aim his rifle &
fire. Saw No. 2 soldier shoot his rifle
at someone in a crowd – a seat in a row of
seats. At me, although he missed the lens, me,
hit only the cameraman whose name I don't know,
who held his camera steady as a mounted telescope
through 1 2 & No. 3 shots. It would be inaccurate to say
he filmed his own death. Even 4 seconds after shot No. 3
I thought the camera would swing around onto a
third person. Even 5 seconds after shot No. 3
the road lurching to a stop *wasn't* footage of death.
The cameraman kept his lens dead centre
right on the cause, the barrel – or bullet
or finger or officer's order or *coup d'état.*
I will not wonder Why? out loud out of
respect for the dead, if not standing on ceremony
above thousands of small white criss-cross crosses,
still respect. I saw the seconds unreel for the first time
7 years after they were news on television news
when I might have been *not* watching another channel
because it was the hottest December night of
the hottest December day for 35 years &
I knew the cinema would be air-conditioned &
because a newspaper listed a wrong time a week before
& I arrived late for Galileo's inquisition
& after complaining to the ticket-seller
& then to the Manager by telephone
was rewarded with a complimentary to any film
of my choice & chose a *realpolitik* documentary
with an army set & wound up long before by Prussians
& still wearing Nazi uniform, including helmet
in a country where women clapped saucepan lids
above their heads in opposition to my hero
going down with a machinegun in his arms
as if it were a camera or Chile.

Dimitrios

1

Twenty years are a long time to know
nothing about someone opposite
just his wife & two sons
Paul who plays the drums &
His Largeness Peter the Large
who was often at large in the street
during his early teens. Now both working.
I wanted to understand, tried to understand
sometimes did understand more
than every second word.
He said he was Greek before he was Jimmy.
There were Greeks here, Greeks there
Greeks everywhere around here
according to Jimmy the Greek.
His lawn was short back & sides
& raking, cleaning & sweeping
to keep the stickiness of
jacaranda mauve away from everything.
After the robots took over his welding
he spent more & more time alone
in his front yard staring into
space or the street.

2

When I entered the church
the Greeks knew I wasn't Greek &
didn't offer me a thin candle to
light & stand in the hanging sand.
I was ushered into a side pew
where I was one of the few
Greeks or otherwise to have
a thin candle lit for
me & for Dimitrios.
In a moment of panic
I thought I might slip out
just as I'd slipped in
but I followed the surge forward &
without kissing the jewelled Cross on the Bible
said how very, very sorry I was
to his widow, his two sons
& at least fifteen people
I'd never seen before
all lined up like gargoyles
along the centre aisle
the only way out for the living.
It was all Greek to me
but I understood
every word.

Section 10

Muesli

Into the cheap white china bowl
I tip a less than usual amount of
a cheap & not so cheap mix of muesli
from a glass coffee jar now coffeeless.
Because the milk in the plastic container
has only three days to go, I pour in
more than my usual quota – although not
enough to bring a lake of milk to the surface.
I empty a bowl of cherries onto the table &
separate the very dark red, almost black
from the still strawberry-red cherries.
After biting & tonguing the stones out of
the very dark red, almost black cherries
I slice them into torn slices of cherry
& sprinkle them onto some fat domes of
cream on special with only two days to go
& now with no days to go but today.
I sit here alone on the cane stool
no doubt enjoying my breakfast
much, much too much.

I'd Join the Revolution – If I Could Find It

I'd pull the cord.
I'd start the revolution –
if it were a motor mower.
I'd join the revolution – if I could find it
flying over the map of the landscape
here, by myself, for a few days
totally hidden by oily summer green
except for the fiddlewood
that's always autumn.
I could find a lover
but it would take a day or two too long.
I could have a Pink Pet or Playmate
to the door within the hour
& fiddle the books.
I could empty the cellar.
My first pushing-forty year old cigarette
though, would see me facing towards the Mecca of
the lavatory bowl. Quicker than dry red.

I nibble away at out of date news
studying the influence of last year on this,
shifting the sprinkler between coups
against salt, sugar, butter, margarine, coffee.
I'm as quiet as a, well, house full of
one. I'm blasted only by the loo
that's not playing rock 'n' roll.
I don't talk to myself. (Too loud.)
I ring the carrot I don't like
& add one to each mouthful of
ham, onion & tomato on toast.
I slice the ham without scraping bone.
Slice the tomato without carving wood.
Take a couple of hours to be
tired enough to go to bed
& not before.
I brace myself for the light switch
going off like thunder.
I do it once, perhaps twice
a year – if I'm lucky.

The Revolution in Coles New World

Not for its own sake but for what it upends
even when the upending is like the upended
even when the upending is upended, I'm
a revolutionary – in Coles New World.
I'm polite & well-dressed. Slow. Calm.
So I'm probably not observed as I observe
the eternal cycles of SPECIALS & PRICE CUTS.
I won't say they revolve; they rotate. True
with only one herb or spice a week on SPECIAL
it takes eons to arrive at the one I want
but I ask myself: would Lenin have dared
to use coriander instead of oregano?
With the most necessary of necessaries
though, I've got the enemy over a barrel.
Even Kings, Czars & Emperors had USE BY dates.
Yellowing tubs of margarine with a few days to go
go down in dollars & cents by two-thirds in texta
as if I couldn't stuff myself week after week.
Old meat with a day or two to go can always
go into the intensive care of my freezer.
I find \$1 off \$2.04 & I've made a killing.
As for all things bright & L'Oréal
\$3 off \$3.99 shampoo & I'm out for revenge.
As if the bottles were a line-up of Romanovs
here goes. I'm wiping out the entire shelf.

Poetic

Even most poets know it. So everyone else
must know poetry about poetry about
poetry is a disaster.

The poetry of slapping flags in the wind
& slogans & leaflets & placards
& partisan spraycans   is

what I'm after when the guns of black pride
are aimed & oiled & pointing at
white South Africa.

Even the poetry of filling a bath with water
hot from gas & kettle & saucepans
during the coal strike   is

even in warm weatherboard houses blacked out
except for two electric lights
allowed on at once   is

the poetry of public speaking's apt tone & gesture
before the largest public audience
in support of the miners   is

the poetry of revolution is what I'd call
poetry if it weren't
a poetic.

Section 11

James McAuley

Third on the national news, he
died of cancer in a private hospital
in Hobart where he was Professor, had
so many books and articles published,
was regarded as a leading intellectual,
a convert to Rome, although he warred
to Australia's north and studied the
South Pacific's sprinkling of islands.

I disagree with almost everything he did
and said, his politics, his religion,
even his private room, but I admire
the way he was able to disagree with
almost everyone and thing, willpowering
himself to keep his faith against
time, logic, history, even geography
in the creed that keeps people alive
by offering another life, no matter
how unlikely it may be.

Judith Wright

Chemical waterfalls drop 200 feet of detergent.
Transmission towers walk in coalseams
stalk the earth as skeletal giraffe or tyrannosaurus.
Some anonymous bird unseen lies tarred by oilspill,
wings fanned in a hand of cards
at poker where its last flight was played
and paid for while cigars turned grey in silver ashtrays.

Observant, though no tealeaf reader, she reads
in her empty cup of black coffee
blank pages, blind eyes
that read no greenery in printers' ink
spilled from printeries into dying rivers.
She abstains from paper for the sake of trees.

Max Harris

His photograph is over-exposed every time
you open those pages like a raincoat.
He's already paid for his tea & coffee
by agreeing with a cruel lampoon of the
two stained tea bags dragging under his eyes.
The silver-topped cane, though, will be
forever *fin de siècle,* too utterly utter &
risky too when he finds Ocker Wildes everywhere.

Still, you have to forgive him his panache
if not his longevity: even as Vegetative Eye
he couldn't have cut in a week or a year
all the trees he's pulped into newsprint.
You can buy banned books he urged unbanning
even at the few bookshops other than his own.
He was early to see chinks in the Iron Curtain not Chinese.
Oh! How he loves Australia. Oh! How he hates Australia.
One week we're all in Sydney; next, on the Nullarbor.
There must be something to be said for a man who's a
non-stop flying neonsign guide to international airlines.
Something. But not much. Still, he tells you how
to avoid your worthy dollars to the Third World
skewered on the Cross with the old Roman Sword.

As a prophet for the 1980s, he foresees
a star-studded future for the 1940s
when he was Mr Jazz, Mr Angry Penguin,
almost Mr Sidney Nolan's Mr Edward Kelly.
Could it be, is it possible he was also Ern Malley?
Predictably professional. Professionally unpredictable.
You could almost believe him if you could
almost believe he believes it, almost.

Ian Mudie

I'm afraid his steep mauve-purple mountain ranges
never reached into peaks of friendship – for me. I was
never impressed by the obvious heroism of heroic journeys
from somewhere through nowhere to sometimes nowhere,
although sometimes from nowhere only to end up
somewhere – all of this exploring, of course. Pioneering.
His snapshots of landscape seem only dull bushgreen
with a bird or two when not sand, gibber or spinifex.
No denying, though, his River Murray and his riverboats.
Who else could have got those old Captains yarning? Not I.
Give me his prose over and above his poetry – almost
any time. His humour over and above his solemnity.

I'm afraid I don't think poets are ordinary people
as he told me they are. Not extraordinary either –
but most extraordinary in their sitting and setting down.
He was most extraordinary, then – those notes going
into his notebooks everywhere he went, why he
lost those lines at traffic-lights on green.

I'm afraid I didn't share his estimate of his poetry-mates,
most of them: could he have *believed* them his equal?
Still, he delighted in catching out the readers of
instant, non-existent books – sounding so credible.
He hated snobs, poseurs, blue bloods and tall poppies.
Wanted everyone to be equal half a lifetime before mine.
I'm afraid I'm both pleased and afraid we shook hands
in agreement over the delusions of the grand leader
we both wanted to win, believed in. But not just then.

I'm afraid I'd give his best prose, his funniest jokes,
all his poems but two for those two poems: the almost anytime,
almost anywhere pain, the red, ageing eyes of 'Chauntecleer';
the almost anywhere fear of what's said behind the back
or thought behind the eyes or thought to be – what's
almost never known, the almost anytime fear of 'The Pursuer'.

I'm afraid he died where I'm sure he didn't want to – in London
although I'll never look at his mountains in the same way again,
knowing his ashes are scattered over the Flinders Ranges.

Flying Colours

She's talking
in the early grooves
telling it any way cocaine
tells it. She's gliding
in, sliding into
high voice
slowly
until
she's
no longer
talking.

She, by herself, is enough.

She loves herself,
makes love to herself
listening to herself
lying before a
record sleeve photo of
herself.

Doesn't she miss
the uncertainty of
another body
another man
another woman?
No. She's intimate
with her own uncertainties of
herself. Alone once
she scratched fire off
a matchbox into
a petal of
greaseproof paper –
not flaming
the dry timber that time
but now flying green & purple
waterfalls of orange
feathers
down
from high up
the wild uplands of
her voice.

Wizard of the Waterpipes

Plumbing, these days, is invisible
and so I'm wizard of the waterpipes.
No harp to play, no wind's strumming across walls,
still I'm king of my castle
master of multistorey.
Mad organist in my tubular cathedral,
I turn taps, fill bowls, pull plugs,
I tinkle and double-bass water and air
down and around clover leaves of plumbing
into expressways of gurgles and chortles and burps.
Excuse me, while I play on my plugs –
torpedo a plastic sub with lethal bursts of air,
while I, er, imitate indelicate lovers five floors down
and while, late at night, after languishing hours,
I manage a deep, building-deep
low-throated lovesong
to my darling thirty floors up,
an eighty year old spinster whom I've never met.
Just for company.

Crazy Mirrors

She's twelve
& the mirrors
the crazy mirrors
mirror her
seventeen
& mirror her
seven.

She
looks for
a long time
at herself ballooning
in the fat mirror. When
no-one's looking she
touches herself & feels
inflated with air
under a thin
peeling of
rubber.
Her hands
are hands of bananas.
Her legs are watermelons.

Then
somehow
she's always
somewhere else
at meal time
or she eats
in her room
where she
doesn't eat
what cats & dogs
will eat or
newspapers wrap &
garbage bins
devour.

She's
nearly thirteen &
fat in the fat mirror
in the fun parlour
she's still
facing.

She
mustn't
overeat
is her reply
to questions
& she always combs
her hair at home
without looking into
her own mirror.

In the
elongating
crazy mirror
she never peers into
she's as thin now
as a pane of
glass.

Statues

What happened to his schoolboy idols?
They were always stilled in statue, immobile
where chisel fixed their rebellion in stone.

Hasn't he murdered them, cracked them now,
laid out the backbone of his race
in a cold clamp of earth? Hasn't he
layered bones to rest in fossil?

Did he see himself in the earth with his heroes?
How can an angle of bones shout
injustice
through time to an ageing archaeologist?

Was his protest the burning rubber
peeling tyres down a slash of road?
Only a car out of control, not him.
See him give his death to the howling crowd ...
that only turns on him in surprise
on seeing his eyes deep-set,
sunken in the rings of a sullen fish
strung up for days in a shop window.

Haunted by wind carving in sand
he caught the posture of heroes
in this century he loathed.

Crowds strike antics around his pose now,
forming themselves, performing their roles
about his broken figure.
Who's to blame them when he, a sculptor,
even into his own hand, chipped his own statue?

Two to the South Pole

Captain Scott –
a man with a fine command of
a Captain with a fine command of
prose, letters, diaries.
His stamina was more than Vitamin C.
He allowed no dogs but dogged men pulling
sledges after horses bogged to their bellies
in snow. Skis an afterthought, un-British.
Only four would go to the Pole. No, five –
a navigator, after blizzards.
Paraffin would evaporate at depots. That's
fire gone from snow-water.
Finding the Pole to be a place
where someone else had been (recently)
while keeping a stiff upper lip (frost-bitten)
Captain Scott set off North, aiming
straight for the sun into sunburn.
Still in command of prose, he commanded
cold, thirst, hunger, festering sores, gangrene.
Oh! Scott was high as the black flag on
Amundsen's tent in his last days dying – high on
what *The Times* would say about Empire
& heroism & sacrifice &
martyrdom & did.

Amundsen took the Antarctic for his palette,
his own ski slope plateau. Made up
games for his men to play –
guessing the temperature.
It seemed like Science.
Over a frozen blizzard of ice-stone,
that ice-row, the Transantarctic Mountains
he followed one longitude only
as if it were a pipeline to the Pole
with four, yes, four navigators
eating his dogs eating his dogs.
Marking his depots with grids,
six miles of black planks on white,
his men urged him on ahead of

his huskies to the centre of the web,
leaving a note for Scott to mail
to the King of Norway – just in case.
Then headed North by night
according to his own Northern lights –
Roald Amundsen, skier, dog racer, ice artist
without an Empire marching behind him
or a fine command of rhetoric.

Christ and Spartacus

Gothic! Grotesque – the God dying for sins, for others.
The man, though. The thorns. The bulk of the Cross.
I wince at a syringe into the rip
between two fingers – the anaesthetic.
Anti-tetanus. Stitches. The rip is shock, mostly.
I can't imagine nails into palms into pain
that's all of life only ending with a life.
And I loathe heavy lifting and carrying.
I take off new sandals when they blister.
I'd yelp for a drop of water He didn't walk on
long before He cried out agony. I'd whinge
and moan and groan until out of voice. I'd
disown everything I'd ever said. I'd say I was
presumptuous, recant, betray, apologise. I'd hope
the soldier would fill the sponge with oblivion.

I wouldn't have lasted long as gladiator
against gladiator's studs, blade, net-tackle,
crated for days' travelling, stiff,
hunched, free only to flex in the arena's
dust like every other upwardly mobile slave.
But if I did tickle an empress's fancy, I'd
use every chance against the impossible chance
I'd ever win even with six thousand slaves
finally crucified along the Appian Way –
rebelling with everything but arms, booty, legions,
hoping that even upsidedown on my cross, I'd die
in my fierce, raucous Freedom cry, Spartacus.

Still, if you can, you do.

One Enchanted Evening

Well, old buggers of sixty
may sunbake in the raw
on their private verandahs
in semi-tropical climates,
may offer sixteen year olds
sherry with the trifle, may
even talk about sending sympathy cards
to imprisoned poofters before it's illegal
to jail them and rightly so too,
by jove, but when they down
too many pre-dinner drinks,
kiss your mother's hand ostentatiously,
abuse the waitress, forget the bill,
lean over you during Oscar Wilde
read from an intimate stage,
you'd have to be very naive
not to expect at the very least
to have your hand squeezed in the back seat
while your father drives the old boy home.
You'd have to expect your good old Dad
to demand you burn the Thank You,
particularly when you open it first,
curious, vain, flattered
while still finding it a bit silly.

An Old Bugger of Sixty

He was an old bugger of sixty
I said, but he wasn't an old bugger.
Strictly speaking he was a pedophile.
Sixty if he was a day, but old?
Well, an elderly pedophile of sixty
sounds dignified, almost distinguished.
With old growing so much older
as I've grown older, how about
an old pedophile of seventy, then?
Any advance on seventy? Eighty.
An old peophile of eighty, then?
At any age he must always be old;
I was sixteen, seventeen. So bugger
it. Why not leave him where he is
to grow old & older & older?
An older bugger of sixty.

The Letter

Found a queer. Put him in my pocket
to flash as conversation piece.

Liked his monologues and jokes.
Always liked a pretty face, he said.

Didn't proposition at first. Asked if he should.
Our recent reading had to substitute.

Rather be queer than straight, he said.
I said Because you're queer.

Had it coming he was so frank, wilful,
nothing could be counted confidential.

Grew in love with a woman – dropped
him cold with my own handwriting

when there'd been no need for words
before I grew up, outgrew puppy love.

I didn't think he'd think it rape, mine,
that penned few lines too many. He did.

Wrong. He didn't know that not writing
proved the more difficult of to or not to.

Always wanting to avoid my own puppy love
I never told him the reason for my words.

He'd unzipped me before I saw
tolerance as a comeon. I zipped.

We're friends now. He's reconciled.
Never mentions try or letter.

I do, virgin, coy not coy I don't know
although not for no one's trying.

Guilt still gnaws through that intolerable note
grinds like bottles up my arse, imagined.

Breaking Into

When you went there, there inside black,
was the black inside speckled with stars –
more than possible to know by
any other means – were you
lighting the way with one of
your favourite effigies of
yourself – simple tallow
& you the burning wick –
black into blue
a metropolis of neon blue balloons
going up like the last of
your oxygen
in bubbles underwater, up
to the bladders of gas full of
black holes
or into black holes disappearing
blue in petal yellow gas – you
blowing them out of your pipe
or inside each one going out of
you, cell by cell

or

was it a hissing a hiss like this –
Mass – my ass, see
it's gas for me
on this umpteenth time trumps
OFF ON OFF ON ON ON
to beat the repeat (no retreat)
this time in rhyme –
this male head dead (hiss)
& this male head dead (hiss).
I'm you & you & you
despite you, to spite you.
I hate you not. I hate you –
you, me, pure sure reckless me
in a hiss & a kiss of
crass gas, I'm me,
finally, me.

Section 12

December Second

If it hadn't been a camera's angle
that framed the bald head
as it rose over the autocue,
ghost of a 5 am sun,
it would have been the hours of long seconds
on a quarter century's waiting
that invested the leader with aura of the spheres.
If it hadn't been for childhood lessons
on the moving of planets as nations
recalled in motionless days,
generations would have come to believe
that one and four faces were one and the same.
Millions could be forgiven, reprieved, absolved,
if they believed that the face in the lens
was the sun's decline
when even the nation's leader knew it was time
to exit on cue.

Don Dunstan's Memorial

Don't name some piquant wine after him
as a collector's item – souring & wasted
antique never to be popped & tasted.
He'd rather you allow a red to breathe.

Don't name any theatre after him.
His song & dance routine was in time
running out across the boards
for old time's sake. Sheer fun.

Don't install a Chair of Poetry after him.
The Union of Poets voted for him anyway
& hardly anyone else could care less.
Those animals at the zoo don't vote.

So finance & design & construct & then operate
a multinational petrochemical infrastructure
with a sickening war record in defoliation.
Half his days as premier disappeared down
the pipes & pipettes & funnels of that
soon to be or about to be working works

he inwardly hated but outwardly had to praise,
knowing no-one lives by life alone.

The Racecall

Over the transistor comes
the hanging up of glasses
by a racecaller I've
never heard of

who, as a kid,

made a studio out of
old pine fruitcases &
never wanted to be
anything else
& wasn't.

Back comes one of the greats he called
galloping fast as Australian turf
& faster around the bend
& into the straight where
jockeys high in their stirrups
call for the whip
on colts & geldings
I've never heard him call
or seen on a racecourse
I've never been to

& I find I'm crying.

Boo hoo!

John

You're a gentleman, he said
as we stood & drank & stood
around the burning drum
in the crowded back yard.
He was standing around
better than I was but I knew
he knew I was listening.
He was a pisspot, he said &
two of his sons were pisspots too &
his daughter was all screwed up.
He said his two sons said
he was a hard man on any man
who wasn't a pisspot too
but it wasn't true, he said
he loved his screwed up daughter
& he loved his pisspot sons
& he loved the son
who wasn't a pisspot.
He loved them all, he said.

Mr Confidential

Everything he says, he says in confidence.
There'd be a lot of gossip, even a conference
if all his confidants found the confidence
to confide his confidences in one another.
Even so, how would they know or find out?
Would it take one to know one & if it would
would it take another one to know another one:
Secret handshakes? Twitching of the noses?
Perhaps I should keep this confidential but
he tells me in confidence his wife is nuts.
It'll come as no surprise to me if he tells
all & sundry in confidence his wife is nuts
mad, loony, crazy, bonkers, round the twist.
I wish I could be confident he'll have the
courtesy & confidence to mention it to her.
I'm not in the habit of sharing confidences but
I haven't been confident about his confidences
since he confided in me he was having it off
with the young mother two doors down the road.
Of course he told me in strictest confidence.
Even if he'd told millions in strictest confidence
I wouldn't have breathed a word of it if he hadn't
needed to apologise to me the following day
for *not* having it off with the young mother
two doors down the road & in all likelihood
not with any other mothers in the vicinity.

Luke's Lost Penis

On the same day Luke's grandmother loses her false teeth
Luke loses his penis. (What's that? False teeth envy?)
Luke might be Lukie to his mother &
Lukie to his long lost father (occasionally)
but he's just plain Luke when he's just lost his penis
which isn't a dick, dickie, thing or thingie
when it's Luke's to lose
but is
Luke's lost penis
which obviously has to be found.
Pointless, a young man going to bed without
his penis. Heaven forbid
he might dream about it –
it or the lack of it. So
while Luke's grandmother keeps looking for her teeth
Luke & his mother look for
Luke's lost penis
in bins
in cupboards
under the bed
until Luke's mother decides
Luke's long lost father is easier to locate than
Luke's lost penis. So, not wanting to
force the man's penis on the young man, Luke's mother
suggests Luke might find his penis in his underpants
where he *does* find his penis – but
it's become unstuck & has to be
stuck back
with sticking tape
by courtesy of Marcel Marceau.

Now Luke's come to like losing his penis.
There are scores of lost penises scattered
throughout rooms & spilling down the front steps.
Luke learns fast at three
minus a bit – years.
Luke's learned how
to lose his penis properly –
cuts it off with scissors.

Front Page

This isn't a movie.
It's a family newspaper.
So 500,000 front page readers don't
see the soldier-sailor's wife's bra
coming, coming off – they see it off
where she's seeing him & he her
for what could be their last time.
She'll take off her bra again
only when he returns from the war,
she says (Many happy returns!)
& if he doesn't return, well,
she won't take off her bra for
anyone else for at least three weeks
& then it won't be a spectacle, just
as it won't be this front page bra
stirring the crane driver to hook
the already unhooked bra delicately
on the steel hook of his steel arm &
lower it like a stork leaving twins
in the arms of the soldier-sailor
who'll keep them under his pillow or belt
while the crane returns to the crane's
inverted question mark, dangling.

Ten Years After

Ten years after
every beautiful cliche
wearing jeans & kaftans & long hair & cheesecloth –
after every beautiful cliche
has gone or may as
well have
for all it means
now
LBJ's gone
& Che's gone
& Ho's gone
& Mao's gone
to their biographers
in the sky without diamonds or LSD.

Ten years after every beautiful demo
that was not beautiful
has broken up
has been broken up
after every beautiful principle
has been broken
has been broken up
after every beautiful principle
that was more outlet &
anger against than for –
pitting the scruffy
against
the grey-arsed men
in grey ties.

Ten years after the most beautiful women
the most beautiful men –
the way they loved
the way they looked at one another after
their long march &
their locked arms straining
& the cops & the charge
& the armlocks & handcuffs
& their heads cracked on duco

& the wagon
& the watch house
& the stench
& together
they'll never forget
even if they're not together
as the candles wrinkle down
around green bottles.

Don't tell me
we wouldn't have cried when Phar Lap died.
Don't tell me
we don't march on ANZAC Day.

Duntroon 1983

They're smearing you with butter.
It's good for you & the National Party.
They're issuing scissors for you to cut the grass –
they're sending you around the barracks for
condoms by the plastic bag full
you'll, they'll never use –
they're standing you to Attennnn Shun
for a full blast fire-hose –
they're ordering you to address the wall
for ten minutes
as Staff Cadetttt Wall –
they're raising bayonets to your throat &
making you Stand Atttt Ease –
they're depressurising your room by
tossing everything not nailed down
into a heap in the centre –
they're demanding tea & sandwiches
in *your* room at *your* expense &
hurling *your* toasted cheese & tomato
at *your* walls & *your* ceiling
until one sticks
like a moving target nailed down, nailed.

Great training for Gallipoli.

Multi-Miners & Co Present Ned Kelly

Multi-Miners & Co present Ned Kelly
as they'll bring you the world's end
unearthing the end of the world
without knowing where to
bury it – ah

inside glass, is it
like Ned Kelly & Co

panning & sluicing for
gold tailings – that's mining

& the iron plough softening
in orange wood coals &
nailed & shaped into armour
front piece, back piece, headpiece –

they were miners who dug iron & legend.

Armour could have been asbestos
if Multi-Miners & Co had known in advance
about the pub fire at Glenrowan.
Imagine the commercials!

Perhaps Ned Kelly was crowned
or, with his headpiece, crowned himself
king of his own Victorian republic,
leading legend off in all directions
when Multi-Miners & Co said they
buried the crown after his capture.

Since 1880 they've all been after
that bulletproof iron crown –
the hopefuls, the get-rich-quick &
the dead, including Lasseter.
Multi-Miners & Co urge them on.

Lay on the legend, they say.
Have Ned coming up out of
a lavender-pink dawn mist
like a robot joined by a
production-line of robots
who then disappear into history
& only history. But keep Ned coming
the Multi-Miners say, keep Ned
coming down to the railway line,
two pistols firing at random – Ned
tilting to & fro along sleepers of
bullets of cartridges of dynamite – Ned
endlessly rocking, endlessly reeling
too slowly to be human
too slowly not to be human – Ned
man & iron man reeling
along the conveyor-belt & on

towards tomorrow & tomorrow & tomorrow.

Leonard

There can be no excuse for you, Leonard:
a life for a wallet of notes
a life & a bit for a few kilometres
a life, a life & another life for a few more.
There'd be an appeal against anything under 30 years
for you, Leonard, if you'd come out pleading
in a hail of criminal justice & a glare of
ghosts only too happy to sentence you
to life in 200 pages. Yours, Leonard. Theirs.
So you finished your own in your own words &
the chase, the arsenal & the encircled farmhouse
woke half the country appalled & fascinated
& envious of your freedom, Leonard, even with you
trapped there in your freedom like a bushranger.
Coffee had a higher lift to it, steaming
up the truth or otherwise of your grudges
the drama, the bravado, the home-made heroism
but you were higher than the coffeeheads, weren't you
Leonard? Under the circumstances it's not surprising
you confused *The Merchant of Venice* with the Jewish Bible
(a pound of flesh for a pound of flesh)
but alone, Leonard, outrun, outgunned, outwaited,
you separated a sociopath from a psychopath
with a single shot to the head.

Pentecostal

Without his God
his Pentecostal God
he would have picked them up
from the strip under the flightpath
& driven them out to the outdoor places
he knew like the back of his hands
the forest, the blackberries
the blue, evergreen river
& before driving them back
with his money filling their next high
under the jetstreams, he
would have fucked them
three times a day
sometimes

but
with his God
his Pentecostal God
he was affronted by them
so outraged by them strung out along the strip
he often complained to his neighbours
before & after he fucked them &
pulled twine or fishing line
or their clothing
tight
around their necks
or
both at once.

The Confidence Man

Knowing your confidence man through & through
gives you confidence in being honest –
even as you lose your life savings.

Envelopes return to the envelopes' address.
The company's photocopier returns to the company.
If you don't become a wowser you'll be a saint.

The dry white & sizzling garlic prawns are delicious
even if you have to shout three times in a row &
his $50 in advance amounts to $150 in arrears.

It's unwise to let his wisdom of delay
delay your sleep, unnerve your nerves as he
tries to turn rat cunning into philosophy.

Your confidence man makes fraud look like incompetence
sticky fingers like just reward for services rendered
alcoholic poisoning like the flush of success.

Every spoken word belies an unspoken sentence.
His promise to repay sounds promising until
the wisdom of delay is wise again.

There's nothing like being more in the know
than contacts, friends, patrons, even lovers
although as the crowd double doubles

to embrace judges, doctors, even premiers
there's more than front in his effrontery –
there's a bearded touch of paranoia

as the man speaks of the confidence man
or is it the confidence man of the man?
Can there be, finally, any difference?

Benjamin

If he didn't pump iron &
tow his boat to the river
he would just appear at dawn
& disappear at dusk
like a water rat.
But he pumps iron &
jump-starts from nowhere
onto his ski &
takes up the slack of
his rope &
zigzags angle after mean angle.
Now & then
his tug of war gives way
to slack nylon & he
somersaults full foetal.
Ready, set, go
in a deep-water start
decades of outboards blast
him up
like a human conning tower
until he's flat out again &
pulling away from any conception of
how much yesterday remains
in today
as he pulls across the wake
high on the power of speeding
& the speeding of power
high on oil & petrol
petrol & oil.

My Ex-Publisher's Influence

I sneeze & not being
a religious gentleman
I don't say Bless you!
but Fatso & Sneezy!
I say Fatso & Sneezy!
almost without thinking
every time I sneeze
Fatso & Sneezy!
the continuing
influence of
the only continuing
influence of
my ex-publisher
my ex-publisher's
long dead cats
on all the hayfever
& influenza of
my days.

One of You

Have your photograph taken
when you're born &
when you're just dead –
& once a year in between.
One of you will be the you
the others are moving towards or
going away from. Don't think
you have to be in your prime
or even make it by forty.
Remember, this is the you
they will remember –
if there are any they
& they remember.

Section 13

Queen Victoria's Diary

In her diary
the young wife
Queen Victoria
liked to watch
every stroke of
Albert's shaving.
As far as it's
possible to know
it's not known
whether or not
the young husband
Prince Albert
liked to watch
every stroke of
Queen Victoria's
shaving or
whether she shaved
at all. It's
equally uncertain
whether the shaving
or not shaving
the watching or
not watching
the recording or
not recording
had more impact
on the rise or
on the fall of
the British Empire.

Pissweak in the 1960s

Michael knew he could be, well, he could be
but this time, *this* time, he wouldn't be.
She was flying from Wellington to Brisbane
but when she landed, she landed at a busy time
for Michael in his fifth year of Medicine.
Although his uncle's farm was about as far
away as it had always been, it was too far.
Returning from the footy he couldn't take her to
for all sorts of reasons all in her own interests
he was broadcasting scrum by scrum over the dinner
he had to take her to (couldn't let her starve)
when his best mate Sam flung back his chair with
Pissweak! & Jesus! or Christ! (or both of them).
Sam told Warwick Michael was pissweak & Warwick
told *me* Sam told *him* Michael was pissweak.
Probably because he was a bit pissed off
even Michael admitted to being a bit pissweak.
So Warwick & Sam & Jesus & Christ & I said
Cheerio & Chin up & Goodbye & Good luck
to the woman who left us standing there
stranded, all pissweak, all weak as piss
all waving from the old airport igloo
Michael waving harder than anyone else.

Difficulties

She's difficult, he's difficult,
they will be difficult
different yet alike.
She hates men, can't
do without, has
to be controlled
hates being.

He wants to be passive, compels
her to dominate, decide,
accept, deny.
She rebels, repelled.
He has to assert
grows aggressive,
gets refused.

All About Periods

Plural, but is one period singular or plural?
The *herstory* of history – *women*struation:
tampons stacked up like cartridges
opposite the frozen peas & fish fingers – much
easier to market than Glad Wrap for wet dreams;
periods increasing the homicide rate, the suicide rate,
the speed & accuracy of dorsal fins;
older sisters warning younger on their wedding days
if not before, not to have *off* periods;
great periods of history – eleven days long;
women bleeding to death in ignorance of periods
or tasting their own blood on a lover's lips;
just plain putting up with periods
or being positively positive about periods,
proud of periods – of tidal power,
of the first man on the moon's *mother,*
the rocket shaped like the – laws of Physics;
women publicly announcing the end of periods;
some women still denouncing periods,
cursing the curse while possessing it;
younger & younger periods in primary school;
Sex Education periods illustrated from Picasso's
early periods. As for men & periods, well –
Hemingway closing his eyes & thinking of bullfights;
Faulkner convicted of importing black slaves
to have white women's periods *for* them – but
released on a good behaviour bond in Mississippi;
this famous nonentity lining up a blood-cult of
seven women in sequence every twenty-eight days,
adding one extra for leap years;
a grandfather writing to the editor about periods
on television between the bloody gangsters & gunslingers;
women replying, attacking, disgusted with poor old Grandpa's
disgust & *not* embarrassed for his embarrassment &
not really expecting Gramps to show much enthusiasm
for women laying down their law of Biology:
Gramps owing his life to periods, period.

Passivity

They're wrong to find me a bastard
closer when I'm their joke
I'm irrelevant more or less
when I want them to win
as they'll will anyway:
liberators of women, mainly women.

Victory will mean losses:
hard and fast rules, hardons
obscene boyblue girlpink
cleaved from birth.
Loss and no loss.

In what I'll gain I regret
depravity's death more than god's,
possession that thrills to a gallery of one
the soul of a stripper
call it hideous or what they will
understanding of the hassled, badgered, assertive,
exhausted, enervated, aggressive
male chauvinist pig's
aching to lose the initiative
jerked or sucked off
passive.

The Best of Times in the Worst of Places

On the ripe day I bought our mango
no-one banged on our locked door.
No cockroach crawled across the ceiling.
The screens kept out all the mozzies
& the rural lobby was tongue-tied.

The ripe idea of buying the mango
might have been more extravagant
than the act of stripping off
its pink, green & yellow jacket
& paring deep yellow flesh down
to fibrous oval seed. Even so

I laid those fillets of pungent flesh
wherever they'd stick in their own juice
& sucked the juice & sweat out of her navel
before we swallowed them soft & slippery
after sharing tangy yellow tongues of
my mouth to hers, hers to mine – sliced mango.

Perhaps I asked. Perhaps not. I don't remember.
After the last slippery slide down our throats
& praying nothing like a prayer, she
took the mango seed in both her hands
and parted my cheeks with a squish of
liquid fibres cooler than a summer breeze.

It Was Sex

It was sex.
Yes. It was sex
but it was arrogance too
they were having
having sexual arrogance. (Lots of times.)
According to him, it was her
making him arrogant;
according to her, it was him
making her arrogant.
At least they knew it was
sexual arrogance they were having
because they'd had sex without arrogance &
arrogance without sex all too often
if never before in a foursome
with each other

& now especially humble & grateful
not having with others what
they can't have with themselves
having had
once
lots of times.

If it's not on, it's not on

If it's not on, there's no point to it
being on, is there? *Ipso facto* if it's off.
Even when it's on, there are those who say
it's off, although there are those who say
it's off when it's *not* on. All depends on
whether it's really on or just on & off.
Since it's possible for it to be off
without being on (a one night stand)
If it's not on, it's not on
must be a polite way of saying
If it's not on, it's not off.
Still, sometimes even when it's on
it's not on – it's both off & not off.
Which puts an end to philosophy.

Dame Margot Fonteyn

Forget about her ridiculous title.
Forget about the two of them strolling
if strolling were ever possible
along the anything-but-secluded
secluded ocean beach – Nureyev & Fonteyn.
While not impossible, very very unlikely
her closest friends tended to think:
Fonteyn & Nureyev, Nureyev & Fonteyn.
So even if you prefer sex to politics
forget about the tutu for a while & meet
the husband not called 'Tito' for nothing.
In Panama it was Right Right, Right Right
& Margot helping 'Tito' to a Left Left coup:
more & more on her tippy toes for guns;
stitching the green & white flag for
'Tito' to raise over Panama City;
in a cocktail dress & high heels zigzagging
around the coast in a fishing boat
away from the end justifying the means of
pistols, grenades, machine guns. Margo
as decoy. If you prefer politics to sex
you could declare 'Tito' shot & paralysed
for a just cause, the cause of the people
(not all of the people, obviously)
when the husband's mistress's husband
might have told a different story.
Margot was in attendance for all of
the twenty-five years it took for
the bullet to find its target –
a Leftie, middle-aged prima ballerina
reinvigorated by a young Tartar
with a fatal taste for boys.

By Your Own Hand

He moves. She moves. They move
but not two as one, moving.
Not jealous, let you
let you not to the rhythm of
two rhythms admit
to your grip
alone & intimate
on one member
& not blind
nor blinding
feel the thread take &
reel like a clot of blood blue
along your arm's vein &
through your deepest-lying artery &
out – unreeling
by your own hand.

Thirty Years After

It is not everything but
thirty years after it was going
to be impossible, I find I'm enjoying
this man's story of this woman & man as I
would enjoy this woman's of this man & woman
(it is thirty years after, after all)
his phonecall from Launceston & she
how he will have to come & see her
in Hobart, but how he cannot & she
how she will drive to Launceston & he
he will leave where he is staying & they
they will go to a hotel room because he
he will have her still screaming at 4am
no alcohol, no nicotine, no dope of any kind
& so still in there time after time
with the timing of a boxer who
knew when to hang up
his gloves.
It is not everything. But.

Stop Grunting

The umpire doesn't grunt
the linespeople don't grunt
the ballboys & girls don't grunt
but the microphones are grunting
your grunts, say the old men of tennis.
A grunt's a grunt & a grunt & a grunt
add up to a double grunt &
a double grunt's a double fault
say the old men of tennis.
If you double grunt your ace or ace
your double grunt with multiple grunts
there'll be no end to your grunting
they grunt, the old, old men of tennis.

The Officer's Daughter

Upheld. The officers' appeal against
her upheld appeal against dismissal.

They won't wear, she won't be wearing
her uniform, revolver, handcuffs.

Before their uniform was her uniform
she'd taken off their uniform for them

as she'd taken on one after another of
them, later, in another kind of line-up

because she'd wanted to be Daddy's
girl & would always want to be.

Caitlin

At least she *wanted* to be a dancer.
Say what you like about Caitlin Thomas
that she was a drunk (well, enough said);
that she was a slovenly housekeeper
(couldn't Dylan have done his share?);
that she aborted Dylan's kids because she
didn't love him enough to have Dylans;
that she aborted other men's kids because
she didn't love them enough to name them
or because she loved them too much to;
that she made Dylan's rage rage death
even worse than his rage rage life
clawing a nun, smashing a crucifix
poking a hole in his oxygen tent
before struggling into a straightjacket.
It probably wasn't, but couldn't it have been
grief rather than excitement at the prospect of
living off the corpse of his royalties?
Say what you like about Caitlin Thomas
but at home with her own gramophone
she'd put on something Isadora Duncan
would have liked to have died to & she'd
dance her way to climax after climax
imagining Isadora. I wish I could.

Tease

When you drool over
two women in high heels
flicking their long hair
back, tongue-kissing
in each other's arms

you have to know it's
more the woman in you
who wants the man in you
on her, under her
on you, under you

than the man on
or under the man

to be absolutely sure
you're absolutely straight.

Section 14

The Woman Speaks

Jesus. How the hell could I
know he was to become a
twenty-one gun saluter.
I liked one two even three. He,
Her representative. How reprehensible
he should grave misdemeanour me.
He. With me. Such a honey too.
Naked, aching for me – my name
another name for variety. But
I wasn't named. *We* weren't
named. I've been called
a four-letter word before
but never a six-letter SINNER.
The disgrace such a disgrace.
Now he's been forgiven. Absolved. But
I won't forgive him his forgiveness.
I don't, he doesn't, we don't
need to be forgiven. Eve or
Mary Magdalene, I see I'm every
man's Everywoman in The Fall –
a fallen woman in The Fall of Man
so we all know he's human.
Such a waste, though, rising
on one and all official occasions
only for the colonial Anthem.

Bob Hawke Replies

If *you* think I'm deliberately misrepresenting
the findings of the Arbitration Commissioner
after the number of times I've already referred
(This hasn't been Hawke speaking but the Commissioner)
to the Full Bench's statements on this & all
other matters concerning industrial disputation
(& in all humility I think I can say I'm
as well versed in the findings of the Commission
as anyone not on the Commission) just for the sake of
currying favour with what *you* call the Right wing
(It used to be the Left, the alleged Left
but I'll refrain from insulting the intelligence of
the viewers by going into *that* particular fabrication)
(Can't you *hear* properly? I said 'fabrication'.
I'll thank you not to put words into my mouth)
if *you* think I'm deliberately misrepresenting
the latest findings of Commissioner Mandala
(Yes, of course I'm using them selectively;
it took Commissioner Mandala a full two hours
to hand down what I might be permitted to call
his perceptive, pertinent & very perspicacious findings)
if *you* think there's any deliberate deception
or disloyalty to the leader of the Opposition
(I've known Bill, now, for at least twenty years)
if *you* think there's been any attempt on my part
(if you'll stop interrupting, I'll answer the question)
to misconstrue or misrepresent the Commissioner or mislead
on this issue or any other issue of industrial disputation

then, you must be *wanking* yourself.

Graham

Hello, Graham, I'm phoning with a
well, it's embarrassing Graham &
I know you'll treat it as confidential.
I can put my trust in you, Graham, I know I can.
The Nobel Committee has just FAXed me (Yes
I've had one for a few months now) the news.
I've been awarded the Nobel Prize for
Illuminated Manuscripts. Thank you. Yes, I am.
But there's a problem. Thank you, I've
always respected your sincerity, Graham
but there is. I've been over & over it.
In conscience I don't think I can accept.
The problem is, well, it's a moral problem really.
After all, there are *other* Illuminated Manuscript Artists.
I'm not concerned about the overseas IMAs
but there are, as you know, Graham
IMAs in Australia, in our region,
even local IMAs – not naming names.
Some of their work is, well, a few of
er, one or two are conscientious & hard-working
& not without a modicum of talent.
What I'm saying, Graham, is that
I wouldn't want to put an end to
all IMA right across the country.
You don't, Graham? I'm very reluctant.
You don't? I really need to think it over.
I'm sorry you've said that, Graham.
It won't take forty days & forty nights.
I will have to think it over
but perhaps I could accept.

Uptight

She's doing her best.
Can't help herself, really.
The backs of her hands scale
red-purple from rubbing.
The palms web a tangle of green veins
through the pallid sheen of
alabaster. No wonder.
She washes them
eighty times a day –
more times than before my time.
Still, I'm pleased to say
I give her some purpose in life
after all her trouble. Lucky me.
We all have our little ways, I know
but taking her own dinner
out to dinner
(her own knife & fork)
is a bit eccentric
you'd have to admit.
She can't eat anything
touched by human hands.
Can't touch human hands
themselves without scrubbing her own.
Can't touch me
without washing herself.
Makes me feel there must be
something wrong with me.
My father was a Lonely Hearts Club man
sent back to the Club
the night after – me.
Not bad for a thirty-three
year old virgin –
although I suppose she
spent hours after in the shower.
I was born in September.
Now she wants another September –
& another & another September
more Lonely Hearts Club hearts
or artificial insemination.

I might be a bit selfish
or the jealous type, you know,
but isn't there enough soap
down the drain here already?
Not mine. I never get dirty.
Don't do anything
much at all, really.
I'm a bit uptight.

Geoffrey Blainey's Facts

A fact's a fact. I'm not against *bad* facts.
I mean I'm against the *fact* of bad facts
but I'm all in favour of your right to
hear a fact called a fact, even a *bad* fact.
Still, I prefer *good* facts. Lots of them.
I prefer *good* facts to *bad* facts. In fact
I prefer *more* good facts than bad facts.
I stand for the rights of minority groups of facts
(outside peak time in languages other than English)
but I don't like whole programs of *bad* facts
chaining Aborigines, branding Kanakas,
feeding convicts on potato peel. No.
What about all the *alternative* facts?
I don't need some Italian immigrant or
the descendant of some Italian immigrant to
mislead me, you & the whole nation on the
mass departure of all non-Europeans at the
founding of the Commonwealth of Australia.
Twenty-two thousand Chinese males remained.
Whether they were too old to travel or
a waste of public enterprise to deport
are matters for judgement, interpretation.
Twenty-two thousand still remained.
There were also three thousand Japanese.
We can't say they spent all their time
yachting & ferry-riding on Sydney Harbour
plotting the best course for midget subs.
Let's be factual. Three thousand Japanese.
As for the vast carrying trade across
the vast tracts of the vast continent –
teeming hordes of Afghans on camels.
Of course we can't give the exact number
because the census takers always consoled
themselves for the tyranny of distance
before they'd finished counting & anyway
they all looked the same. Say, five hundred.
If the powers-that-be only learn bad facts
& never hear about the *alternative* facts
(in fact the vast majority of facts) why

don't they invite *me* to separate the facts –
the noisy minority from the silent majority of
facts. I deal only with facts. That's a fact.

By Days of Wine & Roses

Saw this fantastic movie on tele
the other night – purple handwritin'
stutterin' into life like a jumpin' jack
long as a dragon at one of them Mexican fiestas.
Saw it double – that perfect reflection
in the lake or river or whatever
Minchinbury (& hadn't had a drop).
Just before the skyrockets
shot up & spilled bubbly tinsel all over
the label to celebrate the last letter in the fireworks
the sponsors cut in black & white.
Ya know what black & white's
like in colour. Anyway
this American PR bloke
was floggin' off *Days of Wine & Roses.*
Reckon he bent the elbow a bit
but it wasn't until his wife hit the hard stuff
that it got real disgustin' – I mean
a woman drinkin' out of a bottle.
I got meself a beer
during the next commercial
but by the time I got back
the movie was on again.
Skyrocket shells were bustin' open
sequins of light shimmerin' like (ya should a seen it)
& then comes these great thumpin' capitals
in Commo red over the bubbly
PENFOLD'S
Bloody illuminatin' but I tell ya what
the commercials were a bit off. Still
must get some of that Roses
next time I go to the pub.
The little woman might like a drop.

Crimping

Look, Kayleen, I know you're trying out
a new recipe – but fair go. Crimp me dead.
I can't eat crimp with oysters & asparagus.
I've been crimping my guts out all day long.
No sooner do I arrive home & you crimp my crimp.
Whatever happened to good old fashioned crimp?
For crimp's sake, don't start crimping again.
I mean you can take child psychology too far.
No, I didn't call him a crimping little *chimp;*
I called him a crimping little crimp. Got it?
No, not a *wimp;* I said a crimp. Right? Crimp.
You should be the one to talk. Crimping crimp!
These days you'd rather have crimp than me.
Look, I really couldn't give a rat's crimp.
If he wants to crimp in his room 24 hours
a day, just make sure he locks his door. Ah!
Crimp. I'm too crimped for any more crimping.
Kayzeebaby, I'm not up to the washing-up
yet but, you know, how about a crimp?
Ah! Crimp it. That's all I can say.
Watch out or I'll crimp you one.
Don't tell me to get crimped.

The Gulf Program

Maudie, I wish you could still see the TV.
Pardon? Yes, you've got your transistor
but it's not the same. Seeing is believing.
First I thought the TV was on the blink.
Then I thought it was the ABC. Auntie, eh?
During the golf I saw this gulf program.
Strike me lucky. It was over in a flash.
Spencer or St Vincent or even Carpentaria
I'm blowed if I could fathom it out
but about an hour later it came on again,
another episode, the same but kind of different:
these cross-hairs. Pardon? No, Maudie, sights –
sights not quite crossing a circle in the centre
this bomb with a laser so accurate it bombed
through the front doors, a smart bomb, no,
clever, you know, like the clever country.
Another one went down a building like a lift.
The last one I saw was this bridge, Maudie.
Pow! into one end. Pow! into the other end.
What? Yes, I thought it might be war too
but war without any people anywhere, Maud?
Then it hit me like a bolt from the blue.
The ABC was running commercials, government ads.
They're blowing up *old* bridges & buildings
so they can build *new* bridges & buildings.
Didn't think we'd live to see it, eh Maud?
They've finally done away with the dole.

Princess Diana Refuses to Apologise

In the early days of the marriage, armed detectives burst in on the royal couple making love after Diana accidentally triggered a panic button installed close to the royal bed.
The Advertiser

Don't be ridiculous, Charles. It wasn't
because you couldn't find or hadn't found
the button that I pressed the button.
You had your finger, your tongue &
your, er, Royalty on my button. Ummm.
I like the Royal succession, Charles.
No, it wasn't panic. It was pleasure.
Yes, I could have started World War 3 but
the starlets didn't, the mafia gunmolls didn't
even Marilyn M. & Jackie O. kept the peace.
So don't forget who you are, darling. You
don't have to go to election. No. *Election.*
I know you did, darling. For a few seconds
there we were The Royal We, weren't we?
Well, I could have done without the entry of
the raised truncheons & drawn revolvers but
then again, I've always liked a uniform.
If I disliked all formality, I couldn't
(could I?) ever become the Queen of England.
Really, Charles, I hope you're not going
to go on like this for our whole marriage.
I don't *need* to put a bag over your ears.
All I need do is lie back, shut my eyes
& think of John F. Kennedy. Oops. Sorry.

No Cause for Alarm

Ladies & gentlemen,
there's no cause for alarm.
None at all. Scientists from the
US Environmental Protection Agency
have discounted the claim that giant sponges
90 to 120 centimetres tall, vase-shaped
& thriving on cracked barrels of
radioactive dioxide dumped
into the Pacific Ocean
decades ago
are, in any shape
or form, mutant.

Previously unknown to Science
the sponge is no more than a rare species
adapted to hard & smooth surfaces
that's now in the throes of
population explosion
on the drums.

Bulldozer Driver

Look, I only drive the bloody dozer.
It's 4,500 years old. So what, Prof?
What's 4,500 bloody years? That rock
over there's old as the earth –
it *is* the bloody earth & yer not
dancing the maypole around that, are ya?
Ecological time-capsule. Don't make me laugh.
Look, it's a dirty big hunk of wood.
It *does* nothing. (Birds. Worms. *Grubs.*
Don't give me bloody birds & grubs.
What der ya think the earth's for, anyway?)
Tell ya what, she'd make one hell of a flagpole.
Reckon she'd have in er – awwwww
at least two or even three football stands.
(Crap. I'll Sahara you the bloody Sahara.
Why don't ya take off yer raincoat.)
Tell ya what I'll do when she goes down.
Find yer mate Buddha in the top branches
& I'll turn bloody Buddhist. Fair dinkum.
It'll only take a few more beers. Yeah
& if God shines like a fluorescent tube
up & down the centre of the rings
I'll fix me engine so she won't go
for the rest of the day. Howzzzat?

Benjamin Guggenheim on the Titanic

I'm hardly going to drown my sorrows. So here goes.
Slowly, carefully, deliberately, I'm changing into
my tuxedo. Call it dressing up for going down.
I could do much worse. I have done much worse.
Helping women & children into the boats wasn't
my idea of atonement no matter what people think.
It was the flip side of being a charmer, a rake.
I'm going to die but at least I can say I've lived
even if I have to say it to myself alone in my cabin.
I think most of them enjoyed it & those who didn't
didn't complain. I'm sure I got my money's worth
& I'm sure some of them got my money's worth too.
My money, of course, was worth more than other monies.
My family always stacked my money on the up & up.
Sometimes our tin, lead, silver, copper & diamonds
upped the particular currency right up the up & up.
Old man Meyer would have even bought up icebergs
if he'd foreseen a future in them – or futures.
Well, I'll leave & not leave that to the future.
The cufflinks. The last button. Now the bow tie.

Thomas Hardy Reports on the Raising of the Titanic

Just because you raised it, you think
I've well & truly gone down with the ship
like Keats, stout Cortez & all that. We'll see.
I looked over your salvage & retrieval scheme.
The electronics, of course, were beyond me but
the principles of architecture, hydraulics &
marine engineering are three & the same.
I'll give you credit where credit's due:
V2s, flame throwers, splitting the atom
a cosmology to see & not to see black holes
& spiral galaxies screwing your Milky Way.
Predicting doom was always fun. I thought I'd die
& I was right. I didn't meet my Maker but my end.
I might have taken out poetic licence on my iceberg
but what can you prove with a thin hull that
can't be fobbed off with a thick hide?
Poor design? Find the firm & they'll say
the hull-work was contracted out &
all records went up in the blitz.
If you can pin it on a body corporate
the con man will have worked for commission
proved unreliable, been fired & shortly after
met with an accident in mysterious circumstances.
Of course I was the iceberg. The iceberg was I.
I thought we sank your floating class system
but I was wrong. If I'd managed to be right
every time, I would have been an optimist.
My Schopenhauer might have caught doom & gloom
from what would have responded to penicillin
but be careful what you say about me –
I lived longer than the death of the *Titanic.*

No No-nos

All set, now? Many thanks for coming.
This is the big one, your biggest challenge.
I'm sure you all know the story: globalisation
free trade, market forces, export, export.
No problems. None at all. Just challenges.
Sure, the psychologists were wonderkids.
I could just *feel* those warm fuzzies
as soon as I'd come out of the lift.
Even so, a contract's a contract. B & W.
With your help we won't need them again.
Next – security. It's more than adequate
but we don't need more anymore. We need less.
No, no. Relax, please relax. Jellybeans?
You won't be affected. You're too valuable.
Still it's true, we're downsizing. Have to.
Be positive at all times. Yeses. No Nos
although I want us to agree on No-nos –
fired, sacked, laid off, even retrenched.
You can help them to vocational relocation.
At least *aim* for voluntary separation.
Empathise. Be supportive. But be firm.
A decision is a decision is a decision.
Nothing blunt. Nothing brutal. How about
right-sizing, personnel surplus reduction
re-engineering, workforce imbalance correction
or refocusing the mix of skills & capacities.
They'll know there's nothing personal about
being unassigned, deselected or transitioned.
Of course they're not going to like it
anymore than you will (correction,
sorry) anymore than you would.

Line Manager

What comes down the line to me
I continue on down the line to
them – in a different form.
To keep one of them in check
I invent a process for checking
them all. Call it guided democracy.
For alcohol & even for coffee
they have to open their mouths.
I listen. I keep mine shut
although I keep chatting away.
In a stress claim, I just won't
acknowledge the black & white claims
I've caused them stress & distress.
I stare. They stare back. I stare.
Thirty seconds & they give up.
Unless they go over my head
they have to like or lump me.
I hate them going over my head.
So I go out of my way to go
way over my own head & suck up.
It sucks but it's worth it.
When I have to roll someone
who gets to know me too well, I
look for redundancies higher up &
ease a redundancy into the place of
what becomes another redundancy. Tough.
I promise life & life abundantly
right up until the moment
I have my next in line
bring down the axe.

John Howard Mourns Michael Hutchence

On behalf of my Government I want to say how
shocked & saddened I was to learn of the passing of
one of this country's most talented musical sons.
We've never wavered in our support for Small Business.
The BHP, WMC & News Corp were once small businesses &
so was INXS. They're a credit to their country of origin.
The necessary pressure of quite necessary legislation
that only unAustralian Australians would find unnecessary
prevented Janette & me from inviting INXS to Kirribilli.
I'm sorry. I'm very sorry. I'm very, very, very sorry.
It appears that Michael's last months were his happiest.
In his late thirties he'd found balance, equilibrium.
A family man, he was feeling relaxed & comfortable.
I feel sure he'd have supported my Wik legislation.
How sad, then, his death. It's not for us to know.
Nowadays it's not even for church leaders to know.
Perhaps they spend too much time on moral issues
such as opposing me & my Wik Ten Point Plan. If
only some good could come of Michael's sad demise.
I hope so. Indeed my whole Government hopes so.
It must be obvious to one & all that you don't have
to be poor, drunk, black & in custody to hang yourself.
At 9am on a sparkling blue Double Bay day, you
can be rich, white & famous in the Ritz-Carlton &
still get the hang of it. I'm sorry, I'm sorry but
I'm sorry. Impossible. I can't wear a black armband.
Still, I *would* like to express my deepest sympathy
to all Michael's family (particularly to his parents) &
then welcome Heavenly Hiraani Tiger Lily Yates-Hutchence
to this fine country of mine, of ours, of all of ours.
To make up for your stolen childhood in a small way
Heavenly Hiraani Tiger Lily, I'd feel proud if
you'd accept my invitation to Kirribilli House.
There wasn't much to see when the First Fleet
sailed in, but there's a wonderful view now.

Ivan Milat & Co

Blew em away. Blew *it* away: that murder profile
ya know? Yeah, the one the eggheads had off pat.
Along comes bloody Ivan Milat with his weights
his two buckets of concrete on his steel tube;
bloody Ivan with his marriage & his de facto;
yeah, Ivan with his likin' for women who liked
a man's man who liked hard work with his hands
yeah, Ivan with lots of mates who'd swear by him
& lots who'd swear with him too. My bloody oath.
Ivan buried that profile of a serial killer
somewhere in the Belanglo Forest. Everywhere.
All the eggheads. Yeah, bloody Ivan rooted 'em.
Course, I don't go along with all the sex bits.
Got kids of me own. Don't get me wrong. No way
I'm defendin' the bastard, but if the brainstrust
only had the brains to admit they wouldn't
know a serial killer from a monkey's uncle
they might finally get somewhere. We all might.
Blame? Who's to blame? What's to blame? Beats me.
Fourteen kids, though. I reckon that's goin' too far.
So the Pope's to blame – whichever one it was. If
the calendar & thermometer are s'posed to hold out
against the set square & compass, all I can say is
the rhythm method must be rooted, absolutely rooted
& no sheila had a curette on Medicare in them days.
The abortionists were butchers. Some *were* butchers.
Anyway Ivan was the fifth, not the fourteenth &
who knows? The fifteenth might have been Mickangelo.
If the old woman's blameless, why blame the old man?
A wharfie. A market gardener. The salt of the earth.
Course, he was gung ho about guns, bet ya life he was
but what would ya expect – doilies & antimacassars
to be exported out of the guts of Serbo-Croatia? So
it all goes back to World War 2 like a V2, don't it?
& World War 2 goes back to World War I. Sarajevo.
Yeah, but why did bloody Ivan have to Sarajevo 'em?

Ali Alatas in Jakarta

All these microphones like a bunch of black tulips
I don't know how many television cameras out there
& even more photo-journalists & print journalists –
how could anyone believe I have anything to hide.
The world will not be able to take you seriously.
Your history is a few seconds, a few minutes at most.
Let me remind you we go back many hundreds of years
before the hundreds of years of Dutch exploitation.
We are a most polite people, a softly-spoken people.
Of course we are grateful for offers of assistance.
The Australians, in particular, are always assisting:
joint military exercises, officer exchange programs etc.
There is almost nothing the Australians will not do for us.
No, I have no idea why you would want to say that. Fear?
When will you stop drawing such simplistic conclusions?
There were the ANZACs; now there are the joint exercises.
We find the Australians to be great believers in mateship.
We respect that tradition as we respect all traditions.
So please don't hector us, please don't threaten us.
Don't tell us we have 48 hours to do this, that or the
other because it is just not helpful – to you or to us.
You are ABC. Is that correct? I remember Radio Australia.
When responding to the ABC or any Australian journalist
I always make a point of not mentioning your Aborigines.
I know that you find it distracting & disconcerting.
In my Javanese way I am coming around to your question.
Instead of criticising us & chastising us all the time
you should be congratulating the police & the military
for doing such an excellent job with the referendum.
Yes, it is true there have been one or two incidents
since then. I would be surprised if you were surprised.
The UN tilted ingenuous voters towards independence &
then failed to pin down the voting irregularities. No.
These are nothing but the usual Western fabrications.

Do you *want* to see the Balkanisation of our country.
There may be rogue elements letting off steam (guns)
but the militia is *not* directed by the military.
Pardon? Can I believe what I am hearing? Can I?
You have footage of military personnel on motorbikes
each piggybacking two armed members of the militia.
Yes, they are armed. East Timor is a dangerous place.
Do I need to explain it would be the height of rudeness
for those with transport to leave others to go on foot.
No, you seem to have no understanding of the situation.
The East Timorese packed in military trucks are leaving
because they want to leave. The military are helping.
I have been most patient. This is the last question.
No, not at all. Why would those heading for the hills
burden themselves with huge amounts of food & drink.
I said that was the last question. Well, don't you
always take the children when you go on a picnic?

Down on the Ground

It didn't hit me straight off
only later when I was thinking about
what the old Digger had been trying to say
well, not trying, he'd been saying it all right
if I can just get the words sorted out.
I was doing something at the time
can't even remember what it was
now, but he said he'd had a good life
he had a good wife, a good marriage &
he'd never been short of a bob or a job
but eight-five years later (& this
is what got him – *eighty-five* years later)
he'd been standing there with those left of
those left of his mates & it wasn't as if
he didn't know what was coming but
with the very first one of the
twenty-one gun salute, he
was down on the ground.
TV or radio – I can't remember
but I couldn't get it out of my mind.

Sport News

Good evening. Quite unprecedented scenes today
the first day of the First Test at Nobleman Oval.
Play resumes tomorrow with May on 209, Day on 241
& bowler Nari Narasaravanman still struggling
to complete his first over, still struggling
in fact to complete his first delivery –
the ball No Balled by umpire Buckley.
When the bowler bowled *that* ball again
umpire Buckley No Balled the very ball
that was to rebowl the No Balled ball.
When the bowler bowled *that* ball again
umpire Buckley No Balled the very ball
that was to rebowl the No Balled ball
that was to rebowl the No Balled ball.
No drinks, no lunch, no tea – no way
as bowler Narasaravanman bowled the balls
that were all the way red ball-less No Balls
umpire Buckley No Balling every not-a-ball ball
thereby No Balling all Narasaravanman's balls.
(At stumps Jay Wongar reports from Nobleman Oval.)
Good evening, Fred. An extraordinary day's play.
From the beginning of the No Ball ball calling
the RC & Anglican Archbishops in the Members Stand
agreed to agree No Balls weren't matters of faith.
The Infinite Regress had always been somewhat dicey:
if God caused the universe, who or what caused God?
Who, then, caused No Balls? The bowler or the umpire?
A Buddhist spokesman for the bowling side explained
that little brass Buddhas with little cricket bats
in their laps meant absolutely nothing to his side
but revenue-raising memorabilia for cricket fans.
Buddhists had no problem with no end of No Balls
for they believed in the Nothingness of nothing
from No Balls to infinite ball-lessness of Being.
A Hindu spokesman for the bowling side felt the need
to explain that, of all the world's misunderstood gods,
his Hindu gods were by far the most misunderstood.
Whatever they did, their little cricket bats would be
misconstrued by those aware of the Shalt Nots but not

the sexwork of artworkers or artwork of sexworkers
on the ancient bas-reliefs of Hindu temples & so
their little Hindu bats were on sale as fig leaves.
As for No Balls, Hinduism had always been on about
repeated attempts to arrive at God without arriving
at God. He thought he'd call them Existential No Balls.
(Jay Wongar after an amazing day at Nobleman Oval.)
(Thanks, Jay & I know we're all looking forward to
your new series 'Walking with God, Talking with God'.)
By mid-afternoon the No Balls were concerning Canberra.
The Prime Minister shared his No Balls with his Deputy
who shared his No Balls with senior Cabinet Ministers
who passed on their No Balls to the relevant Minister
who was appalled, disgusted & on the verge of balling.
Discrimination against unfortunates with crooked arms
amounted to ethnic cleansing, claimed the Minister
on his way to two balls – one Greek, one Macedonian.
Relatives of the No Balled bowler should apply for
permanent residency in Australia. The only test
would be their inability to straighten their arms.
Meanwhile the Prime Minister's Women's Adviser saw
the whole day as much ado about nothing. After all
she said, *she'd* never had any problem with no balls.

Putting it all Behind Him

Well, it'd be pointless to deny it. Obviously
it hasn't been the best of weeks for him but
don't forget he was the leading goal-kicker
in the pre-season games – no mean feat for
such a young player. Yes, upset, quite upset.
That's only natural. He thought he was off-air
& he has apologised to anyone he has offended
but really I don't think you'd be surprised
I don't think *anyone* would be surprised to hear
a young player using, well, colourful language.
Possibly, but he has wholeheartedly apologised.
No, no special pleading, no special circumstances.
Even so, he'd attended his grandmother's funeral
only three days before. Overcome, I've been told.
Very sad, yes. Apparently they'd been very close.
She'd given him a football on his second birthday.
From that day on, you know, he never looked back.
That's true, but now he's fit & ready for action.
He took part in all training sessions this week.
A lot of grit & determination – that's for sure.
Oh no, he has well & truly put that behind him.
Yes, he was questioned but no charges were laid.
She did, but then she thought better of it. Yes
she withdrew the complaint. I can't comment but
that's all in the past. Wednesday, from memory
but that's all in the past. No, not a good week
but we're confident it's all behind him now &
he's absolutely focused on Saturday's game.

Bonking

If there's one thing I just can't come at, it's
bonking. Yeah, bonking. Sort of a cross between
ping pong & randy Queensland cane toad. Sort of
like bubbles blown out of a kid's bubble pipe
bonk bonk bonk bonkbonk bonk bonk bonk
nothing bonked into nothing but airy nothings.
Buggered if I can see any point to bonking.
Correction, I can see the *point* of bonking –
it's sposed to take the fuck out of fucking
the screw or screw loose out of screwing &
the shag out of me old favourite, shagging.
I can only say I'm eternally bloody grateful
I never had to bonk anyone in me whole life.
I'm pretty much past it now but in me time
I've known a few bonser little sheilas &
I've always liked to pay em the courtesy of
remembering em. Yeah, I can tell you I've
never forgotten the one with the foul mouth
that really filthy dirty delicious tongue.
I can tell you I used to get all fired up
but bonking. She would have roared laughing.
If I'd had to say to her How about a bonk?
ya know what? She would have tooted the horn
& for once it wouldn't have been mine. Get it?
Betcha do. Ya know, from the way they go on
you'd think ya couldn't get AIDS from bonking
couldn't get old-fashioned VD from bonking
couldn't get bloody anything from bonking
when what ya can't get is something out of it.
Yeah, only one thing worse than a wanker. A bonker.
I've been a knockabout sort of bloke all me life.
I can tell you I'm not easily offended, but bonking?
Struth. It's so inoffensive it's fucking offensive.

Emma on a Rainy Day

It's not raining now but I'm standing
just out of the rain here above the pine trees
waiting for the bus to take me down & around

as a black umbrella, black leather coat &
black old fashioned leather briefcase stops
his full steam aheading (away from lunch?)
& starts full steaming towards me –
not stopping until his full on, full frontal
almost pre-recorded 'I apologise' apologises
& would have whether long lunch or no long lunch
but yes, definitely a long lunch.
I question or half-question why
but we both know why: he lost it
where he shouldn't lose it – in the seminar.
Still, I have to be careful. Okay
I'm more than equal to him right now
but we're not really equals, are we?
I mean we are & we aren't, aren't we?
I give as good as I get, I say
but I know he knows I know he lost it.
Saying it's no excuse, he excuses himself
with the flu. Again & then again. At least
he doesn't say he has a tendency to
repeat himself. He just repeats himself.
Well, if I'm a student, I'm a student.
'I'm not sure how I'm going. How *am* I going?'
The same as he wrote in red, almost word for word.
More clarity, please. He wants more clarity
tripping over three words every sentence.
He has had quite a few glasses, he says
& when I can't help smiling he says
'You noticed'. It's the quote of the week.

Now he's on about chance meetings
about the importance of the unimportant –
the anarchic, the arbitrary, the accidental
the roll of the dice, the flip of a coin
the fall of a raindrop off the tip of a pine needle
if not a special providence in the fall of
a sulphur-crested, white cockatoo.

Will he say I'll remember this meeting
longer than Flinders remembered Baudin
longer than Baudin remembered or
I'll remember Flinders?

No, he won't. Not now, not here, anyway
but he will, he probably will.
So I probably won't.

Post Post Office

Well, there'll always be someone to make your day.
Not old either. Mid-fifties, I'd say. In he waddles
only ever wanting stamps to stick on his envelopes.
What's the point of attending clinics & seminars on
everything under the sun except, perhaps, sex toys
when he waddles in with ten stamps worth of coins &
wait for it – he won't have common booklets of ten.
Still wants the old stamps, you know, the lick-ons.
It crossed my mind that he might be into the glue
but he says he can't get the self-adhesive stamps
off his envelopes if he puts them on incorrectly.
I tried to reassure him but I didn't get very far.
Said you can put stamps anywhere, even on the back
but somehow in the 1950s he must have got the idea
they had to fit neatly into top right-hand corners.
I had quite a run on local postcards the other day
& all the kiddies & even a few of the tourists love
the footballs & cricket bats, the koalas & kangaroos
but now & then you get the odd odd bod waddling in
quite harmless, but making it all so complicated.
Sheet stamps in the 21st century. I mean, really.

Section 15

Upon Upon

Every once in a while you find a whilst.
Turn back. While doesn't live in Whil St
Hasn't ever. Not even Once in a whilst. Still

every once in a whilst you come upon upon.
Say Up yours to the up in upon, if you like;
but don't say comeon instead of come upon.

No matter how many Comeons have been come upon
at all hours of the day & night & night by
livid lovers or wives or husbands or meowing cats

Comeons aren't worth it. Always come upon
Once upon a times even if only video replays of
your long lost one & only one night stand.

You can't keep upon with. But even if you
just keep on coming on with Comeons
you might get your face slapped. Come across.

No! Don't. If you insist on coming down on upon
you'd better make sure of your placard or
someone somewhere will accuse you of violating

the upon in Once upon a time by
spreading the up & the on like legs.

Indeed

Indeed, sometimes all you need is Indeed
under raised eyebrows over walrus moustache
spraying the Indeed out like a waterskier.

Imagine Adam & Eve to Serpent: Indeed.
Archimedes causing the Indeed Stockade.
The simplicity of Marx's *Complete Indeeds.*

Indeed is word. Indeed, Indeed is deed.
Don't take my word. Ask any spy who
learned Indeed as a second language.

Indeed is passé, old hat, decrepit & indeed
what could be better than the last computers
racking their brains to have the last word –

Indeed or its translation in another alphabet.
But if Indeed were lost in translation
you could say, indeed, Indeed is poetry.

So blot Indeed out of the dictionary.
Correct Indeed on the word processor.
Sot or pray Indeed out of the brain.

To avoid However & Moreover & indeed
a hundred galaxies each with a hundred suns
first seen between Indeed & Indeed

cosmologists should take an oath in blood
never, never, never, indeed never to Indeed.

Actually

In a word
actually
in two words
actually is a
British Empire of
a word
a hopeless
hope & glory of
a word
a pomp & circumstance of
a word & world
circumstances
have reduced
to pomp.
Actually, actually
is an in fact word
rather than
a fact
adding
nothing to anything
after or before
the verb
to be.

Lisa

Lisa has a Lisa problem
others have to call Liza
because Lisa is Liza to Lisa.
Calling Lisa, Lisa, only compounds
Lisa's Lisa problem (for Lisa)
although Lisa becomes less of
a Lisa problem for Lisa
the more Lisa sees Lisa as
everyone else's Liza problem.

Don't Say

Don't say
You've never

just say
You don't

& whatever
you do

don't say
You don't say

in reply to
someone

taking you
up on

You've never.

Section 16

Young Mothers

I have this thing about young mothers.
Mine was old, you see. The Second War.
To me all mothers were old until I
grew older than lollywater served by
hundreds of old mothers at school tuckshop.
So I have this thing about young mothers
in the abstract & in the supermarket –
about just about all young mothers.
It is a despicably lustful, possibly kinky,
deplorably one-eyed avoidance of
morning sickness, swollen ankles,
awkward risings from armchairs,
labour pains, prematurity, episies,
not enough milk or too much – the aching,
the lack of sleep, the nappies of course
(everyone knows about nappies)
the colic, the crying, the crying,
the teething, the teeth. So, as I say,
I have this thing about young mothers.
My wife will be an old mother to my son.
Would have been at any age, like me a father.
She is not an old mother – or a young.
We took a long time to get around to it
as they say, as we say (when asked)
& one or two of our reasons were probably
valid. We took – more & more I took.
I have this thing about young mothers.

Who's Who

Hello Graham.
Saying Hello Graham
I'm not talking to myself
in the mirror – I'm
teaching Jeremy who I am –
at least I think I am.
Saying Hello Graham Hello Graham
I pram him, stroll him, bounce him until
I think I'm talking to myself
in my sleep, hanging on
for grim death to my name –
except I'm Jeremy. Must be.
Looking him into the mirror
saying Hello Graham Hello Graham
I've got three heads to choose from –
two of his / one of mine
& he's got two of mine
one of his.

I'm thinking of a committee of psychiatrists
appointing a schizophrenic to compile a
Who's Who Who's Who

& thinking again (although yet again)
about father & son.

This Arm

Creased at shoulder, elbow, wrist
& again between wrist & elbow
as if another elbow, bending

this baby's sleeping arm
as close to weightlessness
as weight can be

as close to rubber as skin;
as close to floating in water
as an arm in air.

Defending Our Shores

We'd had them, but continued to have them–
half a leg or arm of one of the boys
just disappearing through the gate
with his green tennis ball. Once
one of them tried to get away
with the gate chain just for the hell of it
I suppose & a couple of times I'd swear
I didn't turn the sprinkler off, or on.

Now, with a baby just about crawling
out there on the front lawn, you
tend to hear a hard ball hit for six
like a red traffic light. I do, anyway
when the boys had been warned & were
at it again with another one over the top
& this time threatened with parents (hopeless)
& cops (clear the throat, slag)
& for her trouble, she's told she's a fucking moron.
Now *I* don't think she's a fucking moron
or I wouldn't have married her
but I suppose he's entitled to his
even if it's illegal to express it
& No, she doesn't want to press charges.
I'm there the next time one dints the fence
& say Good afternoon ironically as possible
& they shift their game around the corner
where I'm looking for strength in numbers
& find a neighbour's picking me plums
& complaining about their language, such *language.*
The boy's father died a few weeks ago &
he's failed his driver's licence five times
now, but that doesn't excuse his language.
I'm worrying about our dinner parties
& wondering about five centimetre glass
when the ball lands at our feet. No-one
comes looking. Stumps, obviously.

So there's nothing left to do but thank him
for his ridiculous bag of plums, thinking
if this country were ever invaded again
the boys would be old enough to fight
& would want to & would (the excitement)
& anyway, who'd want to entrust
the defence of our shores to
the literati or the intelligensia?

Northern Sunlight

From thirteen months
they're brighter, more delighting
red blue & yellow
in sunlight;
more marvellous
octopus blue
elephant red white & blue
twin bug cars orange & lemon
caterpillar train green orange & yellow
in sunlight –
for a sequin of a second, sequins

but the hand frozen
in the block of ice of the sunbeam
through curtains splitting
northern glass
discovers, invents the sunbeam & the hand
reaching up standing up
on off on course
like a target targetting
down beam white
up beam red
fingers

delighting

as if light were fire
as if light were not fire.

Kindling

The first time I find myself
kindling fire from the fire

the slow boulders rolling nowhere
in their own coronas of flame
in a bed of last night's embers
down now to grey-white flannel
smoking into button-holes of
what will be fire

I'm lying face up on the floor
he's walking (*just* walking
at last at fourteen months)
when he stops at my ribs &
deliberately bends down &
with a wet open mouth
kisses me on the lips
for the first time –
on my lips up to my nose
& almost down to my chin

& off he goes.

I don't wipe it off – I
just leave it on my skin for
as many minutes as the fire takes

just leave it there
not burning, not scalding, stinging.

Flesh & Blood

The thinnest of thin nails
on one small hand swelling into
fingers like a glove
cut to the quick, literally
squirm around their thumb & mine
& through my fingers insinuate
like mud squeezed pink or
mile-a-minute in a pink cartoon
never knotting, never loosening
always plaiting
no grip but gripping
insistently –
when not cutting to the quick.
His mouth stops his bottle.
His fingers could be curling,
un-curling, re-curling hair
that hasn't been cut
yet
instead of
these nerves
five pink nerves –
uncontrollably
my flesh & blood.

Stand Up for Bastards

I've only myself to blame.
I said the wobbling second hand
pine billycart of a cot
was a bastard.
At 20 months he agreed, jumping on a bed,
pointing, shouting 'The cot's a bastard.'
Now just about everything's
just about everyone's
a bastard.
Even a few buggers manage to be bastards.
The evaporative air-conditioner is
the chicken from the takeaway is
the kitchen sink is –
they're all bastards &
I'm the poor bastard responsible.
Irresponsible bastard!
You can see how a meat mallet
can be a bastard bastardising the meat
that's also a bastard bastardised –
a bastard pounding a bastard with a bastard.
But how can knives, forks & spoons
how can salt and pepper shakers
teeter between legitimacy & illegitimacy?
Do away with bastard &
you'll find plenty of bastards;
do away with bastards &
there'll be even more bastards.

The Toddler's Paunch

He fronts up to the long mirror &
pushes up his sweater &
what he sees might be
forty with his corset off
or not holding-his-breath-chest-out
or one of his uncles
pramming & patting his
like a baby – well,
almost like a baby

& (who knows?) when he grows up
he might grow *up* the mirror
like a Jack-out-of-the-box
& the other Jack's beanstalk.

Right now, he thinks he's marvellous.
Pat, pat, pats it like a mud-pie.
Pushes it out & strokes it & laughs.
Goes for his belly button.
Presses – nothing happens.
Twists left, right – nothing.
Pulls, pulls, pulls again
to pull the plug
on air.

Jeremy Remembers His Father

I never had a father.
I had a Graham.
A few bars of *The Threepenny Opera*
never did anyone any harm –
not even at six weeks
he used to say.
He was the proudest of Grahams
when he finally learned off
all four verses of 'The Red Flag'
so I could follow in his footsteps –
all six months of me.
Spending my early childhood
where it would be good for me
in the Early Childhood Unit of the ABC
I don't think I ever saw a woman
in a dress until I went to kindy
& it took me ages to work out why
the men weren't all wearing jewellery.
Of course, I know now why
the sun had to be a yellow balloon
the clouds pulled from cotton wool
the stars snipped out of
throwaway foil pie trays
& why the Star of Bethlehem
would have been an insult to
little Saul & little Yasser.
Once, by pure chance
I pressed the button on *Superman*'s struggle for
Truth Justice & Freedom.
It must have been a bigger moment for Graham
than it was for Superman – what
with his position on censorship
struggling with his positions on
American Imperialism
& Actors' Equity.
While he was raving on
about how *The American Way* of
the old radio serial
had changed clothes into

Truth Justice & *Freedom*
à la Dien Bien Phu *à la* Vietnam
the bird, the plane, the Superman
might have taken only 45 seconds
but it was long enough
for me.
As I heard the thick Eastern European accent
unleash the liquid light down mountainsides
along valleys across plains & prairies
sweeping everything in its path –
small towns, larger towns & on
towards the metropolises & the megalopolises
I saw Superman swoop over liquid light
& hover & hover & hover & then
begin to twist his body
like the blades of a tornado into
a superhuman corkscrew of
almighty suction
& jet
the liquid light
skywards like a rocket
where it unravelled in a nebula
harmless & beautiful & stylised
& fell
in falling stars
anyone could put in his (or her) pocket
calling it a grace or a benediction –
all that, think of it (I did)
just by pressing a button.

The Curls

They're coming off, I'm afraid.
The blond ringlets springing
long enough for a pony tail's ribbon
are sprung, unsprung – can't
outlast his second candle.

His relatives trim their remarks.
Just a bit. Only an inch or so.
The woman feeding peanuts to the monkeys
offers the girl a biscuit. He accepts.
The boys & girls at child care
think he's a girl. Even the doctor
has to confirm a boy's a boy
before lighting up his ears.

I wouldn't side with the short back & sides
if only I could forget that photograph of
Oscar Wilde in a dress at how old?
& how, towards the end
the wallpaper was killing him.

Out of Our Way

We did not take him back
to the one spindling
palm – old black
against the pink of
half a hemisphere of sky over sea

he'd never seen before
through shrubs, fence, roofs, trees of a flat city.

When he asked
we went out of our way
to show him other palms, other skies
but we did not take him back
to that impossibly tall
impossibly thin
possibly dead or dying palm
in that impossibly pink sky –

not even for his fourth birthday.

At Least it's Not Glass

The young lad's doing well for his age.
He already owns an antique wallclock
that improves with age by about a
cent every time the hands go around.
I'll be disappointed if mother
doesn't bypass me, passing on to him
what's left after Animal Welfare.
Quite a haul to tuck into trainers

What can *I* do for the lad?
What better than the dress ring
I had to snip off mid-summer.
An acute çase of baggy finger at 38.
Now, a year later, better stretch it &
pop on. 'It might be yellow sapphire.'
'It might be nothing,' says the jeweller.
'Could we be sure it's nothing?'
Yes. We could. After three minutes
it's rock quartz crystal. I hope
three minutes are too short for alchemy.
'At least it's not glass,' says the jeweller.
'Unusual to have the setting in 18 carat.
More usual around the turn of the century.
Probably English.' He turns up his nose.

I won't take a risk with the undertaker.
'Here we are, son. It's yours. Nothing.
The origin of the universe by
courtesy of god, the father.

And if you turn into a money grubbing
little bastard, flog the gold.'

The Snowdrops

Listen, son,
don't flatten these green blades
don't tramp down these green leaves
don't kick these snowdrops
son, how many more times.
You know I shift the trampoline
twice a day autumn & winter
to keep the sun on them.
Are you listening? You see, son,
the brushfence at the front
lopped off all our daffodils
not even in one big bunch
just more & more
bopped off
each year
until
one

none.

That's why we want to keep these snowdrops
don't we, son? You listening, son?
Snowdrops. They're beautiful
aren't they, eh?
Snowdrops.
Beautiful.

At Five

When I was in Mummy's tummy
you weren't in Mummy's tummy
were you, Daddy? Mummy was.
But how could Mummy be
in her *own* tummy?
(Funniest thing I ever heard.)
How could Mummy *fit* into
her own tummy? She'd
have to cut her head off
or something. Hah hah hah.
And Daddy, how did Mummy
get into her own tummy?
Daddy, *Daddy?*

Parallelograms

As we go where he'll be going, he
heads me towards the big old school that's
no longer part of the small new school.
The sun inlays long windows into a still
polished parquetry floor in a cool hall of
an empty redbrick building. Parallelograms.
The speaker is a black mirror at the
smashed centre of a large grey flower;
the bars & swings & seesaws are movements
to be made from bolts & concrete cradles
from springs & levers set in pipes.
Weeds spindle through bitumen. Angles.
A few low seats remain. All the trees.
Sitting awkwardly close to the ground
ankle-deep in crackling brown leaves,
at least I'm cool in a very warm autumn.
Still live on the main system, the siren
blares hot black wind & glare.

Quartz

He must have swallowed his first tooth.
He didn't have it & it wasn't there.
I don't recognise his second
he holds out to me, crying.
I don't touch it because it looks soft,
don't realise it's hard, a hard chip
until he tells me & it's congratulations
all round & ever so lucky it didn't
go down the gurgler & we'll empty
a glass over it – although
I won't tooth fairy the tooth.
Everyone but the tooth fairy will be pleased.

I've acknowledged my relatives on & off
& off & on my relatives acknowledge me.
(I've even liked one or two of them.)
I've never believed in families –
although I admit now I think of
the hills of quartz crystals pointing
up out of the old inland sea of the
old farm as the rain comes down
like crystals, like light.

I suppose my chemistry & my biochemistry
my geology & my geography are all wrong
but with a flake of crystal now
in my hand from his hand
I can't help thinking, no

not diamond, immortal diamond

quartz, quartz.

The Hypocrite

Yes, son, I know you
learned them all from me
& your mother. I'm
buggered if I was going
to stop swearing
just because I was
feeding you yoghurt
in your highchair.
That's when I swore most.
No, of course I'm not saying
I didn't swear before
you were born. You don't
think I learned them all from *you*
do you? Bloody ridiculous.
I wasn't born yesterday
even if you *were.* Christ!
I know you weren't born yesterday.
I was there. I'm sorry.
Let's get to the point.
You can say anything you like
here. This is your *home.*
You can probably get away with it
in the playground too – depending
on which teacher is on duty.
But everywhere else, son
(are you listening?)
everywhere else
I want you to be
a fucking hypocrite. Okay?
(HYPOCRITE)

Seven

& isn't he proud of
himself, his Cadbury's crayon
all one & a half metres of
yellow plastic striped with brown
around the base of the tip.
He leans against the wall
on the back of his sofa where
he's mastered the art of
blowing it up until
he can touch the ceiling
although mostly he just
holds it in both hands
& points it out from
his body at 60 degrees
& pulls the plug on a
hiss of Yeah Yeah Yeah
through a 150 degree angle
& blows it up again
& rides it down to the floor
like the last moments of
a nuclear family.

Bicentennial Conservatory, Adelaide

Is it a glass-plated dolphin?
Is it a kennel for a tyrannosaurus?
A flying buttress that's lost its faith?
It must be you-know-what when we enter
because my son is Jonah I am Jonah
we're all a democracy of Jonahs
even with only 48% of the vote.
The wooden paths cross in no Cross.
They S & almost 8. That's not infinity.
There are no orders of saints, Sunday morning,
not even the odd ageing nun or priest
to pronounce the botanical species.
All the leaves that aren't burnt
grow in some shade of green –
including the deep green hearts that
who knows? might grow into sermons or miracles.
There are coins in the collection pool.
When the steam floods in like incense
I think of the fire next time –
molten glass petrifying the tropics in a
pre-postmodern art with art object
that would outclass not only Solomon
but the lilies of the field as well.
When the steam floods in like incense
my son looks up from the lower pathway.
I'm standing on the higher pathway.
I think twice about spreading my arms.
It's unnecessary. For fifteen minutes
here, already, this Sunday morning
my son adores me.

Shit

Yes, shit. Not by any other name, it was shit.
Trees thrived on it through old broken pipes
until the loo swelled & swilled over the
top like a bayonet charge in all directions
or the little boy with his finger in the dyke
hallucinating Houdini in a barrel over Niagara.
Actually, it was Archimedes pushing up olives.
The cutter cut through the roots once, twice &
I didn't deny the plumber thrice. After that
it was copper sulphate crystals – or bust.
It was *Root Rid* to be shit rid. Good riddance.
Then I heard it. Shit! Where? Ah shit!

In my son's bedroom. Shit! he said & Shit!
he says when he stubs his toe on his *Lego.*
Shit! he says when he's going to be late.
Losing his sandals is; the wrong channel is.
Constipation or diarrhoea, they're all Shit!
Patience & politeness won't end his Shits!
any more than trying to scare him shitless
by shitting on him from a great height.
Nothing but his days will end his Shits!
I've tried Excreta! I've tried Defecation!
To him they're just more loads of shit &
I'm one great heap of shit. A real shithead!
I can't even begin to tell you how shat off
I am with the little shit Shitting! himself
but after dropping those Excretes! & Defecates!
I can tell you this: no matter how much
the little shit keeps shitting me, I'm
not going to try Sexual Intercourse!

Real Estate

Look, mate
we have to face facts.
I know we live to a ripe old age
these days, but we still cark it. You know
you'll be getting the house & land, don't you?
The land's worth much more than the house.
It's a good area here. Well, a good area
now, anyway. But the house – the house
is only brick & stucco & as for the cracks –
you wouldn't find as many cracks in a saltpan.
The jamming doors. The locks that won't lock.
It's the soil, we've been told. Bay of Biscay.
Most of the places around here are the same
but the bluestone doesn't show it so much.
Renovate & the stone places look good as new.
Even new this place wouldn't have been anything
to write home about. Yes, well, this is home.
I know you've lived here all your life. Even so.
You'll probably want to hang on to the land
but as far as the house is concerned, you
can bring in the bulldozer, the bobcat.
Less than a day's work, I'd say. Sorry but.
Good. That's good. Yes, of course we're pleased
you liked living at home & wanted to stay on.
Cheer up, mate. Come on, think of the land.
I know we've been through this before but
everything has to come to an end
you know, even the earth
even the sun. Aw
come on, mate.

Section 17

Findings

A flat earth.
No. Round.

Round earth.
No. A sphere.

Sun around earth.
Earth around sun.

In a circle.
No. Ellipse.

Rivers.
Glaciers.

Glaciers.
Rivers.

By ellipse.
Off orbit ellipse

& tilt of the earth
tilting more

for ice age winter
ice age summer.

Seas part.
Blacks travel.

Oceans close.
Whites travel.

Whites kill
non-whites.

Not all
says one –

not black
not white.

1988

They're going to fill in Sydney Harbour with Namatjiras.
The whites, the blacks are going to Namatjira the Harbour.
The galleries will take the originals out of air-conditioning.
The private collectors will make their token gestures.
ASIO will computerise the names & addresses of
every newsagent, souvenir shop & novelty counter.
All tea towels, bath mats, ashtrays will be confiscated.
Not a single key-ring or pen-knife will escape them,
not a single transfer onto a toilet roll holder –
let alone a Hong Kong nulla nulla made of balsa.

Every atom of every rock, every dust-mote of every creekbed
that would or could or might have been painted & signed
by the great grand nieces & nephews of the late Albert
will be turned into triple compensation in advance for
not being yet another relative of the once great Namatjira.
The Land Councils will authorise full scale mining of
all his famous hills, cliffs, ridges, ranges, gullies
irrespective of whether there's anything to mine or not.
His stately old gums will be put to the chainsaw.

Won't there be one grown up small boy or girl, though,
somewhere in New Holland, New Portugal or *Terra Australis*
who'll speak up for growing up with a Namatjira print
before Albert became the last of a long tribal line of
English landscape painters no-one wants to know –
least of all the stone Age tradition straight out of
caves into the National Gallery & $200 art books
strongly influenced by twentieth century Modernism
even 39,000 years before Pablo Picasso?

On the 200th year to the day, what will it be –
the heat, the euphoria, the communal champagne
or the piled up debris of all those Namatjiras
that sets Albert walking across Sydney Harbour
like the second coming of the First Fleet

or just some white art teacher's 'Albert Namatjira'
with one old-fashioned nose, one old-fashioned mouth,
both ears intact, two eyes looking dead ahead

no nail marks, no spear in his side, no Cross,
not even the smell of something on his breath,
young Albert walking on millions of old Alberts –
ahead of him, the Great South Land, the island continent,
the inland sea & a whole future of white citizenship.

Deliberate

At the bus stop
a black (male) (drunk)
the white of his whiskers like wire
says Brother, you got a smoke, brother?
Sorry. I don't smoke

but stay at his end of the seat
his & his daughter's – she
fifteen, sober although swigging
from a flagon of white.
Want a drink?
Aw, no thanks.
Don't you drink from bottles?
I don't like it either.
10pm. No.19C.

Talking. Her brother a light heavyweight.
He's almost white. The girl, disdainfully.
The father bums from men
who say No
& women who bypass.

I sit next to right angle seats
so they can talk if
they want to &
do.

He's a certainty at tenpin bowling. Loudly.
Knows how to roll his shoulder.
I'd give you a go.
Challenging me, eh? Loudly.
Finally bums his smoke
but he can't smoke.
Illegal, I say.
His daughter says.
I'll die, he says.

You've only a few more stops to go, I say.
Ding. My stop here.
You'll be right.
Bye.

Tense. Determined. Deliberate as a vote.

Osbert's Voyage

I'd like
to be able to say
that, when Osbert Sitwell
travelled to Australia
by ocean liner
in 1965

departing our shores without
coming ashore –

I'd like
to be able to say
that Osbert was thinking of
Captain James Cook or
Governor Phillip or
even Gallipoli

but I can't.

Section 18

King Ludwig II of Bavaria

It's said that King Ludwig was more
than erratic, artistic, highly-strung.
It's said he was nuts, stark raving bonkers
& not only was he mad, it's said, but he
couldn't be other than mad – all those
castles, castles & a palace for a playpen
all that whim & whimsy & the rolling of heads
King Ludwig at 19 out of the small gene pool
keeping the family jewels in the family
& the story to put reasonable doubt
beyond all reasonable doubt: Ludwig
ordering dinner for twelve, bowing
in turn to each of his guests &
then sitting down alone
except for me.

The Boy

The boy who thought the ward divided
for & against him, who wouldn't eat
behind locked doors & barred windows
if food was served by his enemies, the boy
who duckwaddled to keep his head below
telescopic sights from the next building,
who, when the power blocks blew, said he'd
never be thought an armchair revolutionary
again as he sent telexes to Gough Whitlam
to move the marines faster up river to the city
by using the doctor's reportsheet, the boy
who thought himself on national television
when he broke out through his unlockable door,
his left index finger pointed from bunched fingers
& his right index finger on the trigger of
Assassinate Bjelke-Petersen! the boy who
fanned left to right hand across the ward
before six wardsmen held him down & shot
him 400 mg of eyes uprolled sleeping silence
& 200 mg of walking stupifaction a day –
for freedom through the ward's door & wing's door
& just to clear out of the State at all, the boy
who had to humour all the staff by saying
there wasn't, wouldn't, couldn't ever be a
revolution anywhere or not in hospital anyway,
the boy who had to deny his father's power
with phones in both hands & a dictaphone
& affirm the ward as first rate –
that boy was I.
Is.

The Genes

From how and where I am I should hate his guts
despite his many years dead – my uncle whose
pure gold, large quartz crystal ring I always
wear on my right hand when I'm high or climbing.

He was me as I wiggled my bum for the rest of my
class when the teacher told me to face the board.
The jester, I would be the clown of the class
when not its mini edition walking encyclopaedia.

My uncle and I would either be atop the world
or carrying it on our shoulders. Fatigued. Losing.
I feel I know him only too well. If our uppers
and downers had dipped and risen together, wow!

He died too soon for lithium's magic carbonate.
Nothing to it. Pure physiology. Cells and sodium.
He didn't die. Lives swimming, squirming, spiralling,
squiggling, written on and through the genes of time.

Owed to Lithium Carbonate

Time for the phonecall.
The switchboard operator. Anne.
You're a professional. You like professionals.
So you ask for the Sister; not the Shrink.
You're almost pleased she's at lunch.
Your call returns. The Shrink, please.
Wait a day. Okay. Not bad.
You diagnose. She agrees.
You prescribe. She agrees.
It has already been prescribed.
She does not proscribe. She varies.
Lithium 1 1 1 1 to Lithium 2 2 2.
The Chlorpromazine holding on 100mgs
down to 50 as soon as...
Now, hold out your hands.
Now, spread your fingers.
No tremor. Stiffness? No.
The dry mouth, of course.
Blood test, Monday. See Sister.
May I call you Josephine?
You don't call me Dr Rowlands.
I'll feel more at ease. I'll.
24 hours of urine for the kidneys, please.
Here's the container in a paperbag. Thanks.
Here's the Mood-Chart. Thanks.
(Hope my son doesn't colour it in.
He's pretty manic with his crayons.)

And so to the parachute
on Sister Josephine's wall.
A Lithium Clinic Sister
could be hired or fired for her taste
in parachutes & hot-air balloons.
Not tonight, Josephine. This morning.
What you've pinned up there
is not the tumble from the open door.
It's the moment the body
feels the straps pull
up the down down the up

slow down the down (which was up)
the air filling any cliche
you like to use

always in your lungs &
now in the chute.

You could read every page of
The Ascent of Man
followed by
The Descent of Man
or vice versa

without

coming up coming down with
a better definition of

freedom

Sister Josephine.

The Daffodils

They're not lemon or golden or almost orange, they're
a potion of dye yellow, these unwrapped daffodils
frilling from their most open buds, antique,
their inner cylinders empty, economical.

The same bulbs sprouting in the same place.
In the time & space of one year's turning
again they're all here, bending towards me.
Jacarandas filter light. The brushfence saws off
the sun & they bend south for the other Tropic, straining.

Last year they were shaggy brown wrappings
before I fixed my trance on the fear of red:
bags, vans, biros, fire-extinguishers, anything red.
Even Mars. I ran from nothing. Very extreme.
But stems always opened yellow –
never into dreaming's jets of blood.

After weeks into months of hiding under bedclothes
I open my door onto winter morning's dew.
Everything basks in sunbeams from a sun
like rays on a child's easel, pure yellow.
I should go down on my knees, take off my clothes,
pray to bulb & stem & daffodil & would if
I'd lapped the dew & eaten every petal.

Not that I'm not grateful for daffodils & things:
a floor, a roof, a bed, four fireplaces, windows & doorways,
daily walking to & from butcher, fruiterer, supermarket.
The impossibility of sleeping twenty-four hours a day &
of my life going on without me or me without my life.
Piss, shit, thirst, hunger & dusting day & night.

A social worker. A psychiatrist & his biology & mine
from his arsenal & battery of anti-highs & lows
modulating sodium in & outside my braincells.
No driving. No drinking. Good. A dry mouth. Bugger.

A few friends. Two cats for my wife. My wife
& the dozens of daffodils & I nod our heads & agree
that, by our time, seventy years are many.
Love works a love-change in me at last
as her lips to a daffodil meet mine to a daffodil.

If you can see the sky from where you are &
if it's not sunrise or sunset or a rainy day
what you always see every time you look up
is some shade of blue or the memory of. Now
hold up against this blue, this yellow's daffodil.

On Selling Literary Papers to the Australian Defence Force Academy

for Lynn Hard

Why I *didn't* go to war & all that.
(Failed the medical – probably too one-eyed.)
Then what? My geode. Mexican. Harrods as well.
Rather heavy. Will you pay the postage? Insurance?
My gold chain? When the price is right.
For you or for me? (Never for the blacks.)
How about my house on a CAUTION WIDE LOAD?
Trees? No problem. Pull em out. Put em in.
Shrubs? Why not & bulbs should be easy.
How about $10 a daffodil? $5 a jonquil?
What would you do with my lovers if I
supplied up-to-date addresses of
those still living or believed to be?
Air-freight them in & out on my birthdays
for all angle photographic sessions or
would you make do with once each in wax?
You'll have everyone else. Why not *me*? I'll
give a whole new meaning to Special Collection.
Make sure you make a good offer, okay?
Adjusted for inflation, we'd be looking at
what G.B. Shaw got for his false teeth.

I Know He Knows I Know

Even if he wouldn't have known what to do
behind the lens, he would have wanted to
angle fashion angles at me
clicking whirr clicking whirr
right left right down
straddling me
until we were wet through.

Now I know he knows I know I'm
in my right place behind the lens.
He's performing but he's performing for me.
Done. I hand him his copy of the tape
as if it were his Death Certificate &
watch him in headphones watching himself.
I wonder how long he's got & I wonder
how often he wonders how long.
To like or not to like
never enters my head.
He's too old, anyway.
Still, I think I give an edge to
doing him in before he's done for
if that's what I'm doing when I shoot him
& then file & index him away
although he's silly to give
Death a gender
as if
it were sex.

Repetitive

You've said that, she says & she's right.
Only fifteen minutes before I had
(Dare I say 'said that'?)
Perhaps she thinks I think she's deaf.
Perhaps she thinks I think she lacks
savvy, sophistication or is, in short,
a fool which I don't & she isn't
because not only can she tell
one sentence from another sentence
but one sentence & the same sentence apart.
While not deaf as a post yet, I don't mind
a speaker speaking up a second time.
I wouldn't want to miss anything &
the seconds can provide, well, extra time.
But she's no harder of hearing than I am
as I've already said & I'm saying again.
I'm nothing if not emphatic but I'm

not expanding into the O & infinite os of
the Great Ooooooooooooom of the universe.
Apart from the problem of gravity &
the unbearable heaviness of being 60%
water in the driest State of the driest
(I don't want to state the obvious
although the obvious wouldn't necessarily
be the same us repeating myself)
any repetition of words, words, words is no
foreshadowing or rescinding of the motion
of the earth's rotation & revolution
day & night day & night year in year out.
To Tomorrow and tomorrow and tomorrow I'd
add Today & Yesterday & repeat myself (twice each).
I repeat myself, therefore I am? No. No.
I repeat myself, therefore I am repetitive.
To say. Yes, but ah! To say again.
To underline, to italic, to bold
if I may be so bold as to embolden
even if there are two gas in gaga.

Coffee

If coffee were alcohol, I'd be dead
already. Dead drunk. Drunk dead.
Cup after cup. Mug after mug.
If it used to stop me nodding off
it doesn't now. I'm immune.
A substitute for over-eating
I say to others, to myself
but who'd believe I'm aiming
for the anorexic look by eighty?
I don't *know* why I drink coffee.
Because it's here is no answer.
The aroma, sure, but the taste
only when the proverbial spoon
stands up & says Hi, Old Bean.
If I were a coffee snob &
not the coffee slob I am
I'd be in the red instead of
in the pink of what health
would probably call addiction.
When I buy cheap tins I know it's
going to be vile, but who cares.
My life would have a purpose if
only The Third World made a profit.
I've survived coffee long enough to
have outlived The Great Coffee Scare.
Coffee equals cancer. Boo! Hiss!
None other than the tea lobby
commissioned their own findings.
Even if the dregs were carcinogenic
I'd still say Cheers. Bottoms up.
I wouldn't want to live so long
I'd have to die of everything
when, with a bit of luck, I
can die of something. If not
a long black or it short black
a quick fix, this instant.

The Prince Albert Hotel, Gawler

Only a pub verandah
but high enough for
swallows to dip & glide
in & out out & in in &
under the iron roof zipping
around the old posts &
the new gargoyle – me
way ahead of time again
as I tend to be now
with less & less time left
filling in an hour up here
among the upended pot plants
the old wheel & the guano.
I keep my fingers crossed.
The galah (the one in the cage)
is used to the traffic of
both street & air
but frets, fluffs up &
squarks out a protest
as effective as any of mine
against two bikers roaring
down the verandah as if
it were the bitumen below.
It's nearly time & still
the swallows aren't still.
For a rare & vacant hour
they play through my thoughts.
They're as close as
anything could be
to being my thoughts.
A penny for my swallows.

One Month into Autumn

I'm here & here is in the east of here
looking (I can't lie) north-north-west.
My elephant ears have remained baby elephants.
Agapanthus mauve has gone down its own stem.
The English elm is going gold at the edges.
I don't like the pink of the pink hibiscus
but they pink luxuriantly late in summer
& they pink on pinking on through autumn.
The late sun speckles their leaves into
green rain as it sprays a haze of gloss
or a gloss of haze across the lawn to me.
If I moved a few metres to the west
I could look east & see all sorts of
plants whose names I also don't know
but fascination or laziness holds me here
immobile as the sun plays a yellow scale
up & down the fern-leaf of a fern-frond of
the tree-fern that drinks from the guttering.
In this time & space, at any rate, I don't
think it's possible for the angle of light from
next door to light up the unfolding embryo of
the innermost tree-fern frond. Still
I could be wrong. I sit & watch & wait.
Now the wind is chilling my kidneys & me
but I've brewed a mug of black coffee
so I can draw on & out the yellow light
for as long as I can make it last.

Naming the Season

If I could name the hour
the hour would not matter;
if I could name the day
the day would not matter.
Naming the season, though
would be the mid to late winter of
daffodil bulbs scooped out into flower
the house fluoro-ed in naked yellow
& after the house full of
& the bedroom full of
there would be the vase of
& then the single
yellow periscope
for seeing the last of
the others.

Lythrum Press

WWW.LYTHRUMPRESS.COM.AU